Love That Works

What Others Have Said About
Love That Works

Love That Works *is a wonderfully practical and comprehensive guide to couples' growth—with individual development inextricably intertwined. Jim Fleckenstein – coach, educator, researcher – synthesizes psychology wisdoms and specific techniques into a concise, user-friendly map showing the way to real-life loving relationships. Convenient 'hacks' and topical worksheets focused on common sticking points give readers the skills critical for moving forward, going deeper.* Love That Works *can be any couple's guide to profound intimacy and love, for a lifetime.*

William D. Slaughter, MD, MA

Clinical Instructor in Psychiatry, Harvard Medical School

Love that Works *is an extraordinary resource for clients and clinicians, jam packed with wisdom, warmth, and innovative concepts. An indispensable book in improving relationships. This one goes directly into my clinical library!*

P. Michele Sugg, MSW, LCSW, CST

AASECT Certified Sex Therapist, Past-President, American Association of Sexuality Educators, Counselors and Therapists

Love that Works *is a practical and wisdom-filled handbook on creating just what the title offers. No matter the gender, orientation, and the reader's form of relationship, the book goes to the heart of the core issues that drive all kinds of relationships apart and presents powerful tools that anyone can use to build stronger connections with their partners and themselves. Jim's book draws on the last century of relationship research and clinical practice as well as plain-speak to inspire partners to become better partners. His training program is the kind of bootcamp I would love to send my couples to, giving them hope that long standing patterns that drive disconnection can be recognized by each and how to build safety and communication back into their intimate lives. I am planning on using these worksheets regularly in my clinical practice and I just might use them to do some of my own personal clean-up work in my own relationship!*

Anna Randall, DHS, MSW, MPH

Sex Therapist, Psychotherapist and Sexual Health Researcher

Jim Fleckenstein is a long-time expert when it comes to the topic of creative relationship structures. Jim expands the lens of relationships far beyond the traditional binaries. The principles he writes about in this practical, warm and well written book represent a solid approach to relationships.

Neil Cannon, Ph.D., LMFT

AASECT Certified Sex Therapist & Supervisor, Clinical Fellow, the American Association for Marriage and Family Therapy (AAMFT)

In this readable book, Jim Fleckenstein synthesizes and reacts to the writings of some key researchers and authors, and he includes work sheets for couples to fill out and use as a basis for their discussions on improving their relationships. This book should serve as a basis for directed conversations between those in intimate relationships, with an eye to improving communication and defining healthy boundaries and expectations.

Roger Libby, Ph.D.

AASECT Certified Sex Therapist, author of *The Naked Truth About Sex: A Guide to Intelligent Sexual Choices for Teenagers and Twentysomethings* and *Zipper: A Delightful Glossary of Love, Lust and Laughter*

Love That Works

38 Awesome Hacks for
Amazing Relationships

James R. Fleckenstein

The Earth Moved, LLC
8665 Sudley Road, #132
Manassas, Virginia 20110

James R. Fleckenstein
The Earth Moved, LLC
8665 Sudley Road, #132
Manassas, Virginia 20110
jim@affirmativeintimacy.com
www.affirmativeintimacy.com

ISBN: 978-1-7330394-0-6 (print edition)

Limits of Liability and Disclaimer of Warranty

This book is strictly for informational and educational purposes. The purpose of this book is to educate and entertain. The author and/or publisher do not guarantee that anyone following these techniques, suggestions, tips, ideas, or strategies will become successful. The author and/or publisher shall have neither liability nor responsibility to anyone with respect to any loss or damage caused, or alleged to be caused, directly or indirectly by the information contained in this book.

ATTENTION BUSINESSES, UNIVERSITIES, COLLEGES, AND ORGANIZATIONS

Quantity discounts are available on bulk purchases of this book for educational purposes, gifts, or as premiums. Special covers or other customizations are possible to fit specific needs. For information, please contact the publisher, or use the order form on page 233.

Table of Contents

Acknowledgments and Dedication

There are many people to whom I owe great debts. Listing them all would be an impossibility. On the personal level, I appreciate my family's support and encouragement throughout the years. Professionally, I extend appreciation to my former business partner and dear friend, Carol Morotti-Meeker, MS, MLSP, and to my professional mentor, the late Dr. Robert T. Francoeur (https://tinyurl.com/Robert-Francoeur). Another essential inspirator with whom I corresponded, and to whom much of the credit for my thinking is due, was the late Dr. Albert Ellis (https://albertellis.org/about-albert-ellis-phd/). I also deeply appreciate the collegiality and support of my past and future research partner, Dr. Derrell Cox, II, and of my many professional friends at the American Association of Sexuality Educators, Counselors and Therapists.

I dedicate this book to all the people who are struggling to make their relationships work in an environment that does everything it can to make it practically impossible to do so without selling your soul. Take heart. There *is* a pathway to the successful, joyous, enduring and fulfilling relationship we all desire—and deserve. This pathway lies within each of us, and we need no external guide. We must only learn to listen to ourselves, once we have trained ourselves to

James R. Fleckenstein

discern the truth, and then find the courage to act upon our discoveries.

INTRODUCTION
What Is *Affirmative Intimacy*™?
———————— ♥ ————————

I'm an experienced coach, researcher and observer of relationships. In over 20 years of providing advice and researching how to make relationships better, I've seen all of the common relationship issues. I've repeatedly seen them damage the quality and health of relationships.

I started my journey when my own 25-year marriage ended. The proximate causes were obvious. What wasn't clear to me was how we found ourselves in that position—it seemed to have "just happened." Yet intellectually, I knew that wasn't really possible. Going forward to the next act in my life, I wanted to bring a new intentionality to my relationships. I wanted to know how to do better for myself and for others who struggled as I had.

In my research, I was struck by the diversity of approaches to creating happy relationships. Yet, I felt that nothing I looked at offered a sufficiently comprehensive approach. I felt that many approaches weren't well-grounded in objective research. Others reflected biases that I found unappealing.

I wanted to create a new approach that included the best of the existing literature. I believed it important to ground this new approach in science, not folk tales. It's also important that it emphasize our individuality, diversity and our personal responsibility for our relational happiness.

***Affirmative Intimacy*™** is the result of two decades of research and firsthand experience working with people just like you. This approach is intended to help empower you to create the relationship you want to have. I created ***Affirmative Intimacy*™** to expand on and blend together mutually supporting concepts from the pioneering work of some of the giants of psychotherapy. I firmly believe that if you practice the approach I've developed, you'll definitely see a life-changing positive difference in your relationship. I know it has helped me personally.

Why *affirmative* intimacy? Because it is expressly *not* passive. It puts the responsibility for having the relationship you desire completely in your own hands. Then I give you the tools to fulfill that responsibility. Intimacy and relationship success don't just happen. They require conscious action on a daily basis. But most agree the payoff is worth it!

The ***Affirmative Intimacy*™** approach is built upon four key skill sets or tools. I call them the *Four Pillars*, because they provide the support for a successful, joyous, and enduring intimate relationship.

Obviously, having good communication skills is an essential part of any sound relationship strategy. Communication difficulty is probably the most commonly reported challenge in relationships. I surveyed a wide range of interpersonal communication approaches from education, medicine, business, and relationship therapy—especially those focusing on difficult or challenging conversations—looking for synergies. From this blend, I built the **Structured Dialog** Pillar of **Affirmative Intimacy™**.

Another critical skill that I found essential to successful relationships is a commitment to personal responsibility and a method for stepping back from our emotional reactivity. I drew upon the growing body of research on mindfulness and the field of cognitive-behavioral therapy to develop my own way of helping the people I work with to avoid the pitfalls of some instinctive, but ultimately self-defeating, behaviors. I leaned heavily on the work of Albert Ellis, but once again I tried to incorporate a mix of styles and approaches I found valuable. From this, I created the **Mindful Reason** Pillar of **Affirmative Intimacy™**.

We all enter relationships carrying emotional baggage from our upbringing. This can cause us to slip into comfortable patterns of behavior that nevertheless no longer serve us well. I built on the work of psychiatrist Murray Bowen, and that of psychologist David Schnarch, to pinpoint the critical behavioral lack that hobbles many of us in our pursuit of a good relationship: the socially condoned lack of self-differentiation. Instead of being fully formed adults operating within healthy relationships, too many rely on their relationships to "complete" them, and resort to dysfunctional behaviors to try to get their needs met. This often results in unhealthy enmeshment and equally often in disappointment. Improving one's ability to retain a healthy sense of self while still being a full participant in a relationship struck me as the way out of this emotional cul-de-sac for those I work with. Building on **Mindful Reason**, I try to help them improve their differentiation of self and escape unhealthy enmeshment. The resulting approach forms the basis for the **Differentiation of Self** Pillar of **Affirmative Intimacy™**.

There's an axiom in therapeutic and coaching circles: "you have to meet people where they are." Your work together always starts with the client (and the therapist/coach, for that matter) being where they are in life, emotionally and practically. Before you can make any progress, though, you have to set the stage. You have to lay out a set of goals, a desired end state, and get agreement and buy-in from everybody involved. You can't just rush in and get to work. It's a process that also contributes to trust and confidence building, and hopefully ensures that everybody is on the same page. I've never encountered anyone in the field who disputes this.

Given this accepted need to lay a groundwork of trust before engaging in this kind of emotional labor, I was puzzled and surprised to find that something seemed missing in the work of relationship theorists. They never explicitly discussed this kind of setting-the-stage activity for those who would use their techniques. To me, it seemed that all the gurus and the experts simply *assumed* that the parties who would be trying to apply their ideas were automatically psychologically prepared to engage in these often difficult conversations and activities. This may not be a problem in the treatment room when the therapist or coach is present to mediate, but I felt sure that it could be a problem when clients "tried this at home."

My unique addition was to develop a specific method for co-creating—*in advance*—the **Safe Space** necessary to make progress on building a satisfactory relationship. I feel you must first set the stage and reinforce positive regard for each other before undertaking the heavy lifting involved in doing truly transformational relationship and individual work. I see **Safe Space** as the container within which all of the other skills can be used. Until **Safe Space** is co-created, the best techniques may fall on deaf ears. Therefore, **Safe Space** became the *first* Pillar of **Affirmative Intimacy™**

These are the Four Pillars of **Affirmative Intimacy™—Safe Space, Structured Dialog, Mindful Reason,** and **Differentiation of Self**. Each feeds into and supports the others. Together, I believe they can transform your relationship and your life.

This book is a compilation of some quotations that I've collected over the years that I use to illustrate the Four Pillars principles. They are gleaned from ancient and modern sources, philosophers, authors, psychologists, "gurus," clergy, celebrities and self-help experts. I've complemented them with some of my own reflections and with some action steps or exercises—I call them "hacks"—for you to apply so as to benefit from these principles.

I hope you will find these ideas stimulating and thought-provoking. More importantly, I hope you will find them helpful in building a strong, fulfilling and lasting relationship. I personally invite and encourage you to share your thoughts with me, either directly by email (jim@affirmativeintimacy.com), at my webpage (https://www.affirmativeintimacy.com/ contact-us/) or Facebook page (https://www. facebook.com/ affirmativeintimacy).

N.B. You do not have to have completed my training to use this book successfully. Though I reference my principles as helpful tools from time to time throughout, you generally can still apply the hacks without any formal exposure to my teachings. Becoming familiar with the recommended readings will certainly prove helpful. Of course, it would be much easier and your efforts more effective if you were familiar with my specific approach, and had the benefit of my training. If you're intrigued by what you see here, and are interested in learning more, my website (https://www.affirmativeintimacy .com) is your next stop!

CHAPTER 1
The First Pillar – *Safe Space*
———— ♥ ————

Before anything else can work to improve your relationship, you must co-create *Safe Space.*

Where it fits

As I mentioned before, I found one thing that seemed missing in the work of relationship theorists. They never discussed what must come first before using any of their techniques. Unless you first create a favorable environment in which to use them, they're just ideas. It seemed that everyone simply *assumed* that everybody could just start right in using their ideas without first setting the stage in any way.

Interestingly, some of my insight about setting the stage before launching into communicating even the most difficult news had also occurred to researchers in the medical/pharmaceutical field[1,2] both for patients and caregivers, and in education,[3] but it doesn't seem to have made its way into the relationship counseling field.

So, I incorporated what I learned in these multiple disciplines to develop a method for creating *Safe Space*. Without *Safe Space*, you are seldom able to build an optimal relationship. Until **Safe Space** is co-created, the best techniques can fall on deaf ears. People simply won't take the risks necessary to achieve success if they don't feel safe sharing their truth. Therefore, **Safe Space** is the *First* Pillar of **Affirmative Intimacy**™

It is the foundational principle, the first step in making everything else work. If it's not safe to share *everything*, then it's not really safe to share *anything*, because you never know what's going to be triggering and derail the conversation. Before you can use any other technique to improve communication, process information appropriately, and grow intellectually, spiritually, and in relationship, you have to be operating from a place of safety.

How it works

I identified six elements to the co-creation of **Safe Space** for intimate relationships. (In my trainings, I help the people I work with learn how to ensure these are in place, but anyone can begin to incorporate these into their relationship.) I characterize these elements as creating an *environment*—a place where the alchemy of successful relationships can happen.

1. **Honesty**—*An environment where absolute honesty and transparency is honored, respected, encouraged and expected.* Dishonesty is a deal-breaker. But dishonesty is often motivated by a fear that honesty is dangerous or unwelcome. This fear may or may not be

warranted, but it nevertheless exists. Explicitly removing the barriers to honesty is essential.

2. **Integrity**—*An environment where all parties are committed to personal integrity, self-respect, gentleness, and reciprocity.* This speaks to the open and hidden power differentials that exist in every relationship. Here I work to strip these away and approach the substance of improving our most important relationship as equals, persons of equal dignity and worth.

3. **Non-punitive**—*An environment where all parties are committed to freedom from recrimination, retaliation, and punitive attitudes.* Once again, we seek to obtain explicit consent to put aside fear so as to foster openness and honesty. Actions certainly *do* have consequences, but if we want to get everything on the table so that it can be dealt with appropriately, "gotcha" tactics have to be suspended.

4. **Transparency**—*An environment where all parties feel safe being truthful and transparent, being vulnerable and open, and in trusting their beloved partner(s) with their deepest feelings/needs/wants/actions.* Before we can process anything, we need to know it. A commitment to transparency in sharing our innermost feelings is an essential component of the process. Vulnerability is inherently scary. But having the faith to be vulnerable is priceless.

5. **Mindfulness**—*An environment where all parties are committed to mindfulness (being mentally present and aware) and dedicated to accepting complete responsibility for themselves.* While I talk at much greater length about mindfulness in the **Mindful Reason** chapter, for this purpose I mean stepping away from reactivity and harnessing as much of your rational mind as possible to the task at hand. Foremost in this is always remaining aware that you have sole and complete control over your own thoughts and reactions.

6. **Fear-Free**—*An environment as free of fear, defensiveness, bitterness, dishonesty, subterfuge, or pettiness as two mindful, loving, and well-differentiated people can possibly make it.* This requires an unwavering commitment to approaching even the most touchy topics from a place of receptivity, curiosity, empathy, and love.

If the parties approach matters with these core principles of **Safe Space** specifically in mind, everything that follows will be easier and more effective.

The Trial of Galileo

When a man is penalized for honesty he learns to lie.

~ Criss Jami

If you want the truth (and most of us do—at least in the really important things) it's essential to make it safe to speak the truth. It's funny; we easily apply this principle with the children in our lives, because we always want them to feel safe coming to us with *anything*, but we often seem to have trouble extending this to our partners. No matter how painful the truth may be to us, we must commit to never punishing our partner simply for sharing it. There are, of course, consequences for our *actions*. But what usually inspires us to conceal the truth is *fear*; fear of rejection, fear of being judged harshly, fear of punishment. Essential to a healthy intimate relationship is a climate in which anything can be disclosed without fear of punishment for simply making the disclosure. Wouldn't you rather know the truth so you can shape your actions accordingly, than to remain deceived or blissfully unaware of the truth?

For this to work in a relationship, we must be careful to separate the consequences of *actions* from the consequences of truth-telling. We need to be explicit about this: "I'm troubled greatly by what you *did*, but I very much appreciate your being honest with me about it. Now we can work through what comes next together." Practicing this discipline won't be easy. It will take practice and intentionality. It also offers two important side benefits. First, this practice encourages you to be mindful; it forces you to slow down and consider your thoughts before reacting. Second, and perhaps more importantly, it reinforces for both you and your partner the indisputable fact that nobody is wholly bad or unworthy. By recognizing their honesty and the courage it required, you are forced to take a more holistic perspective on your partner.

The Hack

Reflect upon a time in your relationship when you punished your partner for telling you an unpalatable truth, large or small. How did it feel to you at the time? How do you think it felt to your partner? Do you think that your approach encouraged future honesty, or did it encourage deception and secrecy? What might be some ways that you might have handled it differently? (See "Shooting the Messenger" Worksheet, page 198)

James R. Fleckenstein

Nothing other people do is because of you. It is because of themselves. All people live in their own dream, in their own mind; they are in a completely different world from the one we live in. When we take something personally, we make the assumption that they know what is in our world, and we try to impose our world on their world.

~ Don Miguel Ruiz

Once you grasp this truth, it lowers tremendously the pressure you feel to react strongly and immediately to any disclosure. Grant, for the moment, that your partner is acting in good faith for reasons that make sense to them, however strongly you may disagree. From that position, you are better able to explore each other's realities and learn the *how* and *why* of things, and what the next steps need to be between you to move forward. There *is* an objective reality, to be sure, but each one of us experiences every part of it through the unique filter of our own beliefs, experiences, needs, desires, and circumstances. This is why I teach that co-creating **Safe Space** before any serious conversation is so important—it reminds us that we love and value this person, and they, us. It reminds us, too, that they are separate from us with their own views, beliefs, baggage, and fears. Hopefully this encourages us all to approach even difficult conversations from a place of openness and a suspension of harsh judgments.

In my teaching, I am fond of using the acronym *Q-TIP—Quit Taking It Personally.* Not everything is really about *you*, even if it seems to be. In many cases, what you *think* is about you is really just your projection of your own ego onto experiences or beliefs that your partner is sharing.

Culture tries to instill in us the problematic notion that once we pair up, we become one mind in two bodies, and the longer we're together, the truer that is supposed to be. Hogwash! While it is true that we learn more about each other's habits, beliefs and practices, we never achieve a complete "mind meld." It is not possible nor, frankly, truly desirable. This problematic cultural assumption is demonstrated vividly in popular entertainment. When the "dark secret" is dramatically revealed, the shocked recipient frequently blurts out something to the effect of "I never really knew you!" Well, golly! Where did you get the idea that this kind of complete "knowing" was ever possible? We all have traits and characteristics that are not on complete display, sometimes even to ourselves. These sometimes only manifest in certain circumstances. The point is to step back, discard the unachievable assumption of complete foreknowlege, quit taking it personally, and decide what comes next.

The Hack Can you think of a time when you acted or reacted too quickly to something someone close to you said or did without taking the time to consider, even briefly, *why* they might have done it or said it? What was the outcome? Were you happy with the results? Do you find yourself taking these situations personally? If reacting without pausing to think is a habit of yours, take some time to consider whether it serves you well. If you find that it does not, what is your plan to go about it differently in the future? (See "On Different Worlds" Worksheet, page 199)

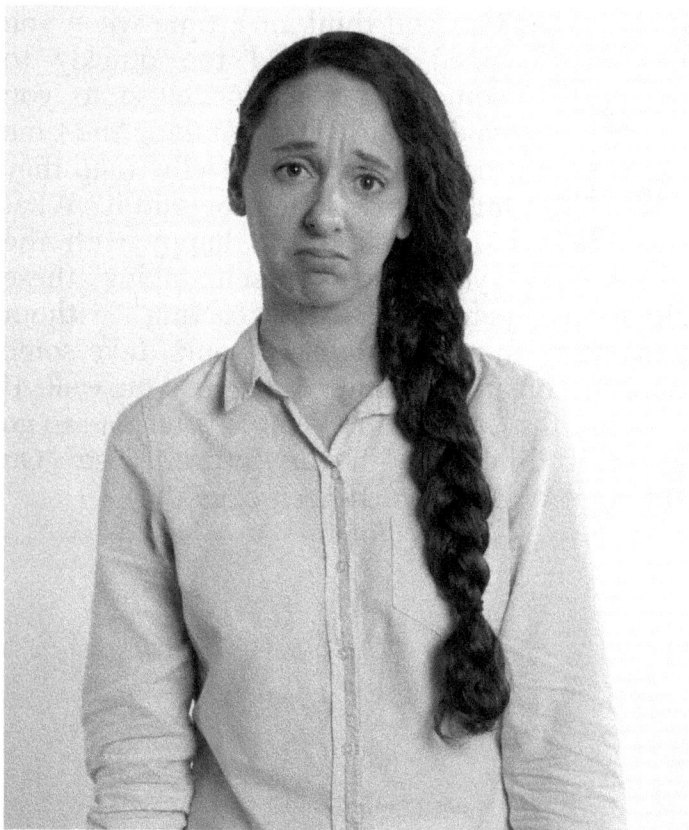

I love you, and because I love you, I would sooner have you hate me for telling you the truth than adore me for telling you lies.
~ Pietro Aretino

When viewed in this light, accepting the consequences of truth-telling is clearly the more courageous act of personal integrity, and can come from a place of selfless love. You can't build a healthy relationship on deception and concealment. We know that intuitively, but when the cost of truthfulness is perceived as too high, it can be hard to muster the courage to be honest. We must move past fear-based relationships that rely on "spinning" the truth to keep the peace. We should strive to move toward a healthy relationship that trusts that the partners have an adult ability to process truthful disclosures in a mature and measured way.

Obviously, nobody likes to be hated. But this quote captures the essence that if one cannot be truthful in a relationship, then there truly *is* no relationship. I'm not talking about the "little white lies" that ease social interaction (*e.g.*, "Sure, boss, that tie looks great!" or "I'd love to do lunch on Friday, but I already have other plans." (when you don't)). These are relatively harmless, though it would be better if they weren't necessary. What I'm talking about here is the need for a more-or-less constant state of deception around subjects deemed "too hot to handle." The real danger lies in that dishonesty will metastasize like a deadly cancer and will consume the relationship and the people in it.

The Hack

Quick, what's your initial reaction to this quote? Do you agree that truth-telling is more important in a relationship than flattery in the long run? How do you handle situations when you're faced with this kind of choice? How would you *really* like your intimate partner to handle such situations? Beyond social niceties, do you agree that "honesty is the best policy"? Or do you find yourself more comfortable with "what they don't know won't hurt them"? If the latter, what do you think has caused you to feel that way? Can you identify specific instances, or is it a more generalized fear? Can you develop a game plan to challenge your thinking on this topic and adopt a more forthright approach going forward? How do you plan to do this?

Speak when you are angry and you will make the best speech you will ever regret.
~ Ambrose Bierce

Heeding this simple piece of folk wisdom is one of the most important steps you can take to improve your relationship. When the emotional temperature is too high, honesty and transparency melt away. Worse still is when the increased temperature transforms everything said into an attack or a defense. Following the carefully planned steps of co-creating *Safe Space* *before* the temperature rises in an exchange can prevent a great deal of regret. It's hard not to let emotions take control when we run unprepared into a conversation that "pushes our buttons." That said, we have a responsibility to ourselves and to each other to do all we can to prevent that from happening. The people I've worked with find that taking the few extra steps involved in co-creating *Safe Space* beforehand can help to keep the emotional temperature of the conversation at a comfortable level, no matter how significant the subject matter.

Many sage experts suggest taking a time-out when the emotional temperature gets too high. While I fully agree with that, doing this is like using a fire extinguisher. I much prefer fire *prevention*—taking steps ahead of time to keep things from getting out of control. These include developing a more mindful approach in general, and specifically going the extra mile to set the stage before entering into a difficult conversation. If such a conversation couldn't have been anticipated for some reason, and the resolution of the situation is not time-sensitive, then by all means step back and schedule a time to have the conversation when both of you are better positioned to achieve real results.

The Hack

Do you generally try to hold your tongue when you're angry? Do you let your anger get the better of you and find yourself frequently blurting out things you later regret? What skills do you think you'll need to improve your ability to step back from your angry outbursts? How do you plan to gain them? If possible, ask for your partner's support in agreeing to defer difficult conversations under circumstances likely to prevent either of you from using best practices. Jointly develop a system of simple code words either of you can use to indicate that a conversation needs to be deferred; perhaps a simple "green-yellow-red" will do. Yellow might mean "I just need a little time before I'll be ready to discuss this more calmly," whereas red might mean "I really want to defer this matter until we can set an appropriate time and place to have a rational conversation." Be creative in setting your code words; if they can be somewhat humorous without being corny, that also might help to defuse the situation a bit.

We know from our experience that it is easier to develop trust in another person or in a group if we believe that we can disagree, and we will not be abandoned or hurt for our differences. It is difficult to trust those who deny us the right to be ourselves.

~ Susan Wheelan

Too often, our conversations are controlled by our fears and apprehensions about how our messages will be received. One common reaction to this fear is self-censorship, which almost always leads to a destructive secrecy. Secrecy, as contrasted to a healthy sense of privacy and personal boundaries, is almost always corrosive to a relationship. Yet secrecy and lack of trust are unfortunate natural consequences of a perceived lack of the safety to be transparent. When we treat the fundamental uniqueness of our partner as a problem to be solved, as opposed to celebrating it, we set ourselves up for barren and lifeless relationships. If every difference is treated as a tragic flaw worthy of ultimatums, scathing attacks, or emotional abandonment, you can be assured that your relationship will never provide the nurturance and sustenance you need to grow and thrive.

The key to this concept is maintaining a sense of proportion. Some differences really are insignificant in the long run. Trust comes from a belief that differences are ok, expected, and only rarely showstoppers. This is not to suggest that "anything goes." But unless we are prepared to accept our partners, warts and all, we risk losing the relationship.

The Hack Maintaining your personal integrity, and allowing your partner to maintain their own, is essential for trust and mutual respect. Reflect upon a recent situation where you had a profound disagreement with your partner over something significant. Did you continue to feel fully connected to them despite your disagreement, or did you find yourself withdrawing or distancing? Can you identify the reasons why you believed withdrawing was the right response? Upon examination, do you now feel those reasons were valid and growth-supporting? If not, how might you respond differently to such disagreements in the future? (See "Withdrawing" Worksheet, page 200)

James R. Fleckenstein

The use of tact is always needful but it is especially necessary when speaking a truth that may strike a sensitive nerve in another.

~ Robert E. Fisher

Nothing I recommend or believe suggests that anything other than the utmost care and attention be given to maintaining an appropriate gentleness in our approach. While some advocate an "unvarnished truth-telling," I am not in that camp. There is no place for harshness or a lack of appropriate regard for our partners in the process of truthful exchanges. In fact, the entire concept of co-creating ***Safe Space*** together is to ensure an emotional climate that retains due consideration of our mutual support for, and importance to, each other.

Tactfulness can consist of making sure your communication is not shaming (how *could* you...), universalizing (you *always*...), or disrespectful. It is about choosing the appropriate time and place for communicating, ensuring there is sufficient time and privacy for a meaningful dialogue to occur. To some extent, it is about "picking your battles"—avoiding needless conflict over minor matters. Tact is *not* an excuse for withholding or evading the truth, or for clumsy attempts to "soften" what must be said. Rather, *tact* is a mindfulness around the possible sensitivity of what must be discussed and an open-hearted effort to be gentle and considerate while never sacrificing truthfulness or personal integrity.

The Hack

Do you feel that you better understand the difference between tactfulness and deception or evasion? Could you explain it in a sentence or two? Try writing it out, and keep at it until you're satisfied you've got it. If you're having trouble with this, I invite you to step back and imagine some scenarios, real or imagined, in which you could be tactful yet wholly truthful. How does that feel to you? Is the difference clearer? I also ask you to recall a couple of instances where, in hindsight, greater tact was called for than what you displayed in reality, and then to think about how you might proceed differently in similar circumstances in the future. (See "Tact vs. Deception" Worksheet, page 201)

James R. Fleckenstein

Fear is not in the habit of speaking truth; when perfect sincerity is expected, perfect freedom must be allowed; nor has anyone who is apt to be angry when he hears the truth any cause to wonder that he does not hear it.

~ **Tacitus**

Be honest with yourself. Have you acquired the bad habit of having a "short fuse"? Have you failed to develop the personal self-confidence and resiliency that allows you to hear the truth—even difficult or unpleasant truth—without excessive reactions? If you need to work on this set of skills, the **Safe Space** techniques I teach will prove an important starting point in managing your reactivity. Excessive reactivity (which also manifests itself as a symptom of a lack of differentiation of self) usually comes from a place of fear and personal insecurity. We sometimes try to stop the "bearer of bad news" by becoming "that touchy person that everyone walks on eggshells around." Do you see how damaging this personal characteristic can be to an honest and open exchange of information? Your (perhaps unconscious) attempt to shield yourself from discomfort or from having to confront or accept things you would rather not is preventing you from knowing things you really *must* know!

There's an old saying that makes the rounds in various forms: "When you get to be archbishop, you'll never want for another meal again. But you'll never hear the truth again, either." Like too many bosses or officials of every stripe, if you've made it unsafe to share with you, you in fact have no right to be angry or upset when the inevitable negative "surprise" brings your world crashing down around you. I find that the process of co-creating **Safe Space** will lead you in the direction of being more approachable and better prepared to cope effectively with whatever comes your way.

The Hack

Can you recall a situation (at work, at home, within your family of origin) in which your denial of someone's desire to be truthful with you ended up blowing up and being even *more* hurtful to you and that person down the road? How did that feel to you? Can you think of a time when *you* were the person with an important, if unpleasant, truth to tell and you were shut down by the person who needed to hear that truth? How did that feel?

If you agree that the feelings engendered by sensing that you've been unable to be truthful, or to hear an unpleasant truth, are problematic, what specific steps will you take in order to do things differently as either the giver or receiver of such messages in the future? (See "I Don't Want to Hear It" Worksheet, page 202)

In order that all men may be taught to speak the truth, it is necessary that all likewise should learn to hear it.

~ Samuel Johnson

If you want and expect your most intimate relationship to be characterized by honesty and sincerity, both of you must learn to speak *and hear* the truth calmly and without excessive reactivity. We're not taught to do this very well. For example, while the *telling* of truth is always emphasized in raising children, we don't do anywhere near as good a job at teaching them how to *hear* the truth. In fact, we often encourage children—by our example—to be very *bad* at hearing the truth. We grow up not knowing how to accept complete honesty, and we seldom expect it, much less demand it, from our intimate partners. We feed each other "gentle" untruths and thereby get in the way of each other's growth and development.

It will take time and some concerted effort to unlearn this damaging and immature habit. The payoff is definitely worth it. With reliable (though tactful) truthfulness, trust can blossom between you. You can contribute to each other's complete development as a mature and resilient individual. For yourself, your ability to accept the truth from a place of inner strength and freedom from self-imposed fears is priceless. It grounds your relationships on the bedrock of mutual strength rather than the shifting sands of trying to compensate for each other's developmental weaknesses.

The Hack

Think about the practice of truth-telling within your current relationship. Is it truly mutual, with each of you free to speak your truth—with tact—when called for, or is there a conspiracy between you to avoid it? Even worse, do you expect to be free to speak *your* piece without constraint, but are reluctant to extend that courtesy to your partner? Reflect upon opportunities to build a respectful, equal balance of truth-telling in your relationship. After carefully thinking this through, try to involve your partner in a discussion about *their* perceptions of the state of truth-telling and truth-receiving within your relationship. If this conversation reveals opportunities, work together to agree upon some concrete steps to improve matters. Agree on a reasonable future time to check in on your progress, and to make needed adjustments.

James R. Fleckenstein

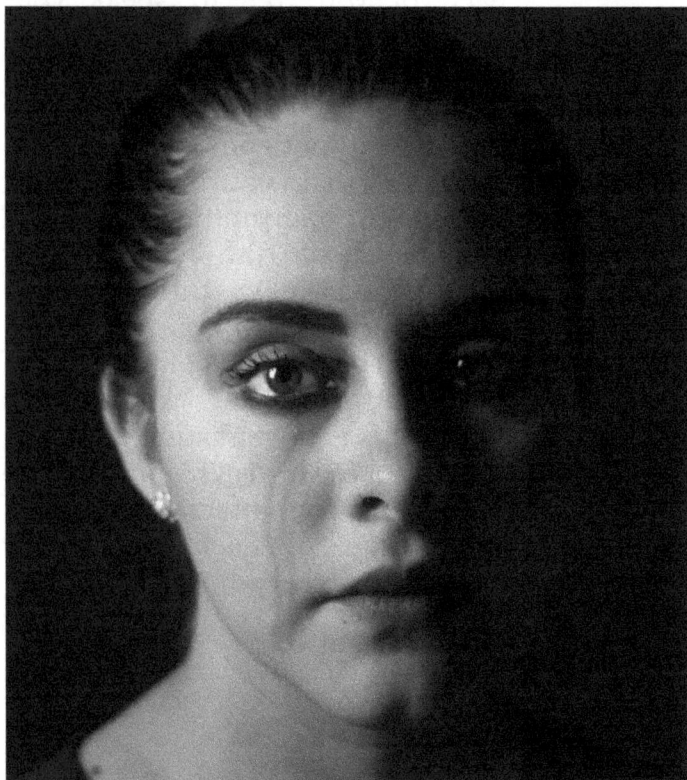

More information is always better than less. When people know the reason things are happening, even if it's bad news, they can adjust their expectations and react accordingly. Keeping people in the dark only serves to stir negative emotions.

~ **Simon Sinek**

Uncertainty and concealment are *never* your friends. Our active imaginations will fill in any blanks in our understanding, usually with the worst possible explanations! This in turn breeds frustration and resentment. Concealment, even if arising from the best intentions, disempowers your partner and disrespects their autonomy. Few of us appreciate being on the receiving end of concealment, yet we are often only too ready to resort to concealment ourselves. Finding the healthy boundary between appropriate privacy and dangerous secrecy can be challenging at times. Popular culture abounds with injunctions about complete transparency. Every failure of this recommended transparency is dubbed "infidelity"—financial infidelity, emotional infidelity, infidelity via pornography, etc. I'm completely on board with healthy openness and tactful candor. I'm opposed to sacrificing all our privacy and individuality on the altar of an unhealthy "togetherness." Once again, it is about finding balance and a sense of proportion.

If you or your partner have difficulty with avoiding overreaction and emotional outbursts, the task of providing appropriate levels of disclosure becomes harder. I find that applying the techniques of co-creating **Safe Space** will help. By providing explicit reassurance and recommitment in advance of the conversation, the process helps defuse some of the fear, defensiveness, and unhealthy reactivity that are the implacable enemies of authenticity and open dialogue. Over time, using these techniques reduces the incentive to conceal the truth or evade openness about emotions, beliefs, and actions.

The Hack

Can you recall a time when somebody close to you deliberately withheld important information from you? How did you feel about that? Did that experience create closeness and harmony or did it foster distance and discord? Did that person's motive for withholding this information make much difference to you at the time? Can you recall a time when *you* were the withholder? Can you recall your rationale for trying to conceal the information? How does this rationale feel to you now? If these experiences were problematic or unpleasant, or had bad consequences, what are your plans to avoid this behavior going forward? How do you think you can enlist your partner's involvement and support in putting these plans into action? (See "Withholding" Worksheet, page 203)

James R. Fleckenstein

When we speak we are afraid our words will not be heard or welcomed. But when we are silent, we are still afraid. So it is better to speak.

~ Audre Lorde

Fear wears many masks. The masks our personal fears choose to wear vary with each of us, but the end result is usually the same—a measure of emotional paralysis. As Lorde so eloquently states, though we are afraid to speak our truth, refraining from speaking it does not relieve our fears. It is better to bring our truth out into the light of day and abide the consequences than to suffer the self-inflicted pain of concealing it within. Sometimes, we know our fears of disclosure are well-founded. We will at times find our disclosures unwelcome or deliberately unheard. That's ok. The process of attaining freedom from the fears that keep us back takes time and application, even in the face of difficulty.

Fortunately, this kind of truthfulness doesn't require your partner's participation, though of course mutual efforts at growth are more likely to succeed and have lasting effects. Many times, you will find that your fears were baseless, and none of the terrible outcomes you so dreaded actually happen! The first step is for each individual to confront their fears and try to strip away the masks so as to reveal exactly what it is that is so threatening. Only then can we begin to confront and defeat these threats. Suffering in silence does nothing for our partners or ourselves. I tackle this challenge in part through the ***Mindful Reason*** Pillar as well. As noted previously, concealment only encourages the growth of "emotional weeds" that choke out the blossoming of an open and equal relationship.

The Hack

Reflect upon a time when you felt you had something vital to share, and yet for whatever reason felt too afraid to speak out. How did you feel about that experience? Is this a feeling you're eager to have again, or for those close to you to have? Can you identify what made you feel afraid at the time, and whether that fear ultimately proved to be justified? What specifically do you intend to do to help reduce any climate of fear and withholding that may currently exist within your relationship? (See "Speaking Your Truth" Worksheet, page 204)

The one charm about marriage is that it makes a life of deception absolutely necessary for both parties.

~ Oscar Wilde

Wilde's wit has a barb precisely because we know it to be too often true. A lifetime of social conditioning can render us vulnerable to living a "life of deception" within our relationship. This may give the outward appearance of a calm and functioning relationship, but in reality it creates a powder keg of suppressed emotions just waiting to explode. Some people are able to sink into a state of sullen discontent and endure for years or even decades. Others engage in guerrilla warfare tactics, hiding behind sarcasm, snide remarks, or unceasing criticism, eventually provoking an explosive reaction or even a breakup. Still others find themselves increasingly living parallel lives, yoked to a life partner they know less and less about, and share less and less with. Does any of this sound familiar? Do you know people who fit these patterns? Could they even describe your *own* relationship?

I believe it is obvious that none of these patterns of coping with the presumed need for deception in a relationship are healthy or promote personal growth and well-being. Clearly, there are many situations in life where complete candor may not be the best course of action, but there should be vanishingly few such situations within your most intimate relationship! Each opportunity for openness that you pass by— usually out of fear—adds more powder to the ticking time bomb. The process of co-creating **Safe Space** begins to break through the wall of "benign deception" that erodes real trust and prevents you from having the unfiltered communication essential to a healthy and sustaining relationship.

The Hack

Have you ever known a couple who seemed locked into a perpetual struggle of criticism, sarcasm, and put-downs? Have you ever known a couple who have stayed in relationship for many years, yet rarely seem to interact beyond social niceties? While these characteristics may be more common in past generations, we definitely still encounter them today. "Living together alone" is a melancholy description for too many relationships!

Do any of these traits sound familiar to you in your own relationship? Have you or your partner fallen into habits of deception and evasion that have hardened over time? If there's even the slightest familiarity, reflect upon what specific steps you will take to help wash that approach right down the drain!

James R. Fleckenstein

CHAPTER 2
The Second Pillar – *Structured Dialog*
————— ♥ —————

The way you choose to communicate can do much to determine whether your communication succeeds or fails.

Communication is a critical skill in every method of personal and relationship growth I studied. It's also one of the most frequent trouble spots reported by individuals and counselors alike. I *had* to include communication education. Though based in part on the work of psychologist Harville Hendrix, I also blended in important insights from many other specialists in difficult interpersonal communications.

Fortunately, there is a great deal of research on how best to communicate, and the many reasons why we so often fail to communicate well. My task in creating the ***Structured Dialog*** Pillar of ***Affirmative Intimacy*™** was to put together a streamlined, effective approach that fit in with and enhanced the other Pillars.

Where it fits
After you've co-created ***Safe Space*** in which to operate, you must devote your energies to being

sure you are communicating effectively. The **Structured Dialog** process seems terribly cumbersome and awkward at first. You're compelled to spend a lot of mental energy on the process itself in the early stages. But once you begin to master the concept, two important things happen. First, the process becomes less awkward and more natural. Second, the rewards become increasingly obvious and are a strong source of positive reinforcement.

Over time, you'll be so used to the process that you'll gain the ability to use shortcuts with each other that achieve the same results. If something really becomes a sticking point for your communication, you may have to revert to the detailed, step-by-step approach to get past it, but such instances should become increasingly rare.

Clear and accurate communication between partners helps set the stage for applying the next Pillar, **Mindful Reason**.

How it works

Hendrix identified three process elements or steps to effective communication: *Mirroring, Validating,* and *Empathizing.*[1] In *Mirroring,* you listen without judgment, repeating what the other party said until they confirm you have correctly understood it. You also make sure you've got all the relevant information. In *Validating,* you make it clear that you understand how your partner might feel that way. It's the "can you affirm I'm not crazy?" step in the process. Finally, in *Empathizing,* you put yourself in your partner's shoes and affirm that you understand where they're coming from—the *why*.

Importantly, none of this means you must agree with the *substance* of the message, but it ensures that you truly understand the message, and assures your partner that they have been heard and understood. Then you have set the stage for a productive conversation about the substance.

James R. Fleckenstein

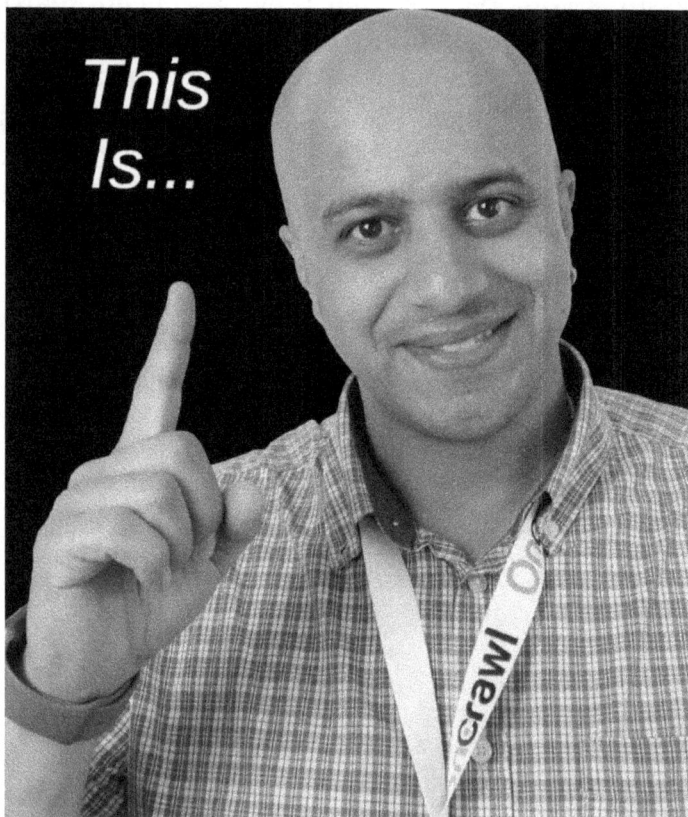

When we name things correctly, we comprehend them correctly, without adding information or judgments that aren't there. Does someone bathe quickly? Don't say he bathes poorly, but quickly. Name the situation as it is, don't filter it through your judgments.

~ **Epictetus**

One of the hazards of unplanned communication is the tendency to be imprecise. This starts a cascade of unintended consequences. You're not sharply focused on what you really mean, and your listener is put at a disadvantage in understanding. They, in turn, share back an equally imprecise response which you then misunderstand or misinterpret, and the conversation quickly spirals downward. Again, in the real world, not every exchange needs to exhibit razor-sharp precision. But lazy or imprecise thinking leads to imprecise communication, which it is wholly within your power to avoid. This is especially important in critical or difficult conversations.

Beyond mere imprecision is the tendency to incorporate judgments in our choice of words. As Epictetus points out, incorporating our judgments into our statements "spins" the thinking of both the speaker and the listener. This hurts communication, and can create conflict where none is intended. These judgments or "spins" can be subtle, reflected in our choice of words or even our tone of voice. They can operate below even our own radar, unconscious artifacts of our upbringing, life experiences and beliefs. The **Structured Dialog** process that I teach can help reduce this problem by slowing down your communication a bit, helping you to be more mindful around what you intend to say, and then using a back-and-forth process to help increase the chances you and your partner will be correctly understood. Effective communication depends on accuracy and as much precision as we can possibly provide. Whether you are able to use my process or not, "Think before you speak" should become your mantra.

The Hack

Going forward, try to catch yourself inserting implicit judgments into your descriptions or statements. Do you simply state the facts, or are you prone to "editorializing"? Make a brief written note of each time you find yourself doing this, and what the general subject of the conversation was. These don't have to be extensive, just enough to serve as a reminder to you. Over time, look for patterns. Are there topics that seem to bring this out in you more frequently? Is it a general habit, one that colors many, if not all, of your conversations? Try doing this for a month or two.

Once you've gained some insight into when this situation occurs, you are empowered to work on dropping the judgments from your descriptions of circumstances, events, and people. Continue the practice of keeping brief notes and review your progress from time to time.

Discussion is an exchange of knowledge; argument an exchange of ignorance.

~ Robert Quillen

For many reasons, it can be easy for a discussion to become an argument. In a discussion, we are seeking to understand and be understood. In an argument, we are seeking to be acknowledged as correct and to defeat the views of the other person. Which would you really rather have? To keep your conversations on the high ground of being discussions rather than arguments demands mindfulness and some effort. Arguments often happen because either or both parties are intellectually lazy, unwilling to put in the effort to keep focused on understanding. The misunderstandings that occur as a result frequently trigger our defense mechanisms. We feel attacked or put down when perhaps there was no intent to do so. We feel unheard or disrespected because real communication isn't happening. We gain no real knowledge, but rather fall into the trap of reinforcing our ignorance.

The ***Structured Dialog*** process drives out intellectual laziness by helping all parties to stay focused on achieving understanding. It takes away a lot of the "tripwires" that can transform a discussion into an argument in an instant.

Following this practice, or something like it, keeps all parties to the conversation engaged in true fact-finding, which in turn occupies the "mental space" that might otherwise be devoted to experiencing anger or frustration.

The Hack

Does this ring a bell for you? If you frequently find discussions sliding into arguments, what do you think is the cause? Are there commonalities in the topics, time of day, etc., in the discussions that don't go well? If you see any patterns, write them down. This exercise is supportive of the previous one. Whereas the previous exercise is simply to detect "spin," this one is to identify when your discussions devolve into arguments, regardless of your use of "spin." Taken together, you may find commonalities that can be most enlightening.

After tracking these situations for a time, give this matter some serious thought; what might you do to avoid repeating these patterns? How can you implement a plan to avoid getting locked into "exchanges of ignorance"?

James R. Fleckenstein

Two monologues do not make a dialogue.

~ Jeff Daly

How many times in your life has real communication become impossible because the parties were talking past each other? Both are focused only on being heard, and not on hearing. When this occurs, there is no chance that communication will take place. I see this often in couples' repetitive arguments over the same issue; the issue never gets resolved because both simply continuously restate their own positions.

Another style of monologuing is when one partner simply dominates the conversation. There are many causes for this; some are reflective of socially-constructed gender differences – men tend to speak longer than women once they have the floor[2] – while others result from unhealthy behaviors like withdrawing from difficult conversations. Regardless of the cause, when a conversation is not reasonably balanced it can be due to one or both partners' monologuing habits.

There is a wealth of literature on active listening. One frequently encountered pitfall in achieving good listening skills is the practice of *thinking ahead;* that is, diverting our attention from the ongoing conversation in order to formulate our responses to what has been said. This practice sabotages our attempt to fully understand what is being said, and is a prime cause of monologuing. Though this is a naturally occurring habit, it is one that you must be especially on guard against if you want to achieve real communication in your relationship.

The Hack

Take a look at the last couple of arguments you've had without reaching a resolution. Can you remember in detail your partner's key points? Could you reverse roles with each other and successfully advocate each other's positions, even if you disagreed with them? If you're not sure you could, then you (and/or your partner) could be subject to the tendency to monologue.

The next time you find yourself in an argument that seems perennial and non-productive, ask for your partner's cooperation to pause the conversation and try this technique. If you can't do it, you need to work harder on truly listening to each other! Even if your partner doesn't agree to try this, you can do it on your own after the fact. Like so much else, if you can improve your *own* functioning, it inevitably will work to improve that of your partner! (See "Did I Hear You?" Worksheet, page 205)

James R. Fleckenstein

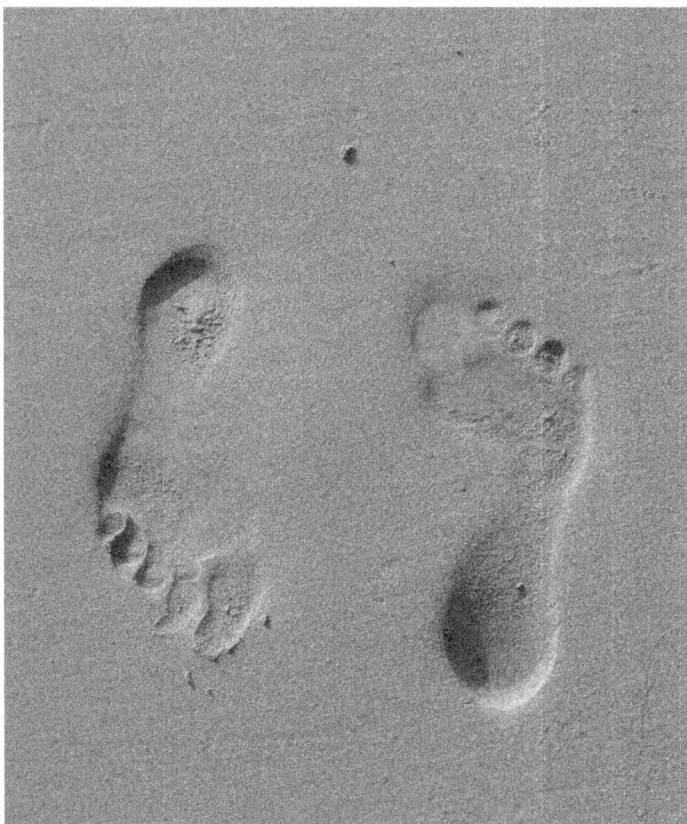

The single biggest problem in communication is the illusion that it has taken place.

~ George Bernard Shaw

When we communicate poorly and aren't mindful about it, we often find that what we *thought* we had communicated was never actually received. Monologuing is a big contributor to this situation. Failing to check in and confirm that not only was your message "heard" in the sense that your partner knew you said something, but that your message was *really* heard in the sense that it was fully understood, is a prescription for trouble! When couples present for help saying "we just can't communicate," this phenomenon of *believing* you've communicated when you actually haven't is often the culprit. We all lead busy lives, with many demands on our limited attention. It is tempting to "dash off" communications, whether verbally or via electronic media, and expect the recipient to fully understand and act accordingly. This may be ok for inconsequential things, but then again, how many bitter arguments have ensued over someone's failure to execute a simple task like picking up the dry cleaning on the way home?

At its most basic level, **Structured Dialog** is expressly designed to prevent this from happening. The steps involved force both partners to really listen, ensure full understanding, and confirm this to each other. It prevents intellectual laziness and substituting assumptions and guesses for genuine communication.

The Hack The next time you have a conversation with your partner about something substantive and concrete (not a philosophical or abstract discussion, *e.g.*, politics, the latest Facebook post, etc.), take some time afterward to write down privately the main points you were trying to make to your partner and you believe you communicated successfully. A week or so later, without advance notice and at an appropriate time, ask your partner if they would be willing to try to convey back to you what those points/action steps were, while you check against your contemporary notes. How well did it go? Did your partner get 80% of your message? 50%? 10%? After discussing the outcome, ask your partner to cooperate by reversing roles and trying this again (without revealing which conversation is being monitored). This exercise should serve to highlight how well (or poorly) each of you is currently communicating/listening, and identify opportunities for growth. (See "Did You Hear Me?" Worksheet, page 206)

James R. Fleckenstein

If you understood everything I said, you'd *be* me.

~ **Miles Davis**

When you look at it this way, it all makes perfect sense! Too often couples in relationship, especially longer relationships, fall victim to the fairy tale notion of "one mind in two bodies." We come to believe that we can predict our partner's every thought and belief, and therefore can be excused from doing the work of seeking to understand them. This assumes that your partner is fixed and unchanging, and that every situation you encounter is just like something you may have encountered in the past. The shortsightedness of this approach is apparent, but it's one of the most common "communications" issues I encounter. We are *not* mentally joined at the hip, and never can or should be! Remembering how one's partner prefers their steak done can be endearing, but believing that a partner's reaction to a challenging situation or circumstance can be confidently predicted can be a prescription for disaster.

Nothing ever excuses each of you from the responsibility for truly communicating. Being present, speaking clearly, confirming understanding, and validating viewpoints are never optional if you hope to achieve real communication.

The Hack

The next time you find yourself thinking, "Why didn't he/she *know* that?" or "I never knew she/he liked *that*," stop yourself and make a mental bookmark. Examine why this lapse occurred. Were you *assuming* something? I understand that not everything in our inner lives must be an open book to our partners, but too much concealment can lead to problems.

Recommit to sharing your thoughts and feelings with your partner, inviting them to do the same, and refraining from expecting them to read your mind. Keep being mindful about this and notice if the incidence of these experiences is diminishing. If not, map out some concrete steps to increase mutual sharing. Perhaps try a periodic, playful session of "Did you know…" in which you both share something you believe your partner didn't know about you, but should.

James R. Fleckenstein

Remind yourself that if you think you already understand how someone feels or what they are trying to say, it is a delusion. Remember a time when you were sure you were right and then discovered one little fact that changed everything. There is always more to learn.

~ **Douglas Stone**

Wise counsel indeed! There is always more to learn, and if you seek to understand and be understood, you must always remain committed to learning more. Jumping to conclusions and/or believing you already know what your partner is saying—or trying to say—are prescriptions for *defeating* communication, not improving it! As Stone correctly notes, sometimes that one little missing piece of information can change your whole viewpoint, but you'll not get it if you don't seek it. TV crime dramas rely on this kind of plot twist all the time. It works because it is realistic. Our minds are somewhat pre-programmed by evolution to jump to conclusions—there isn't always time to evaluate calmly whether that sound from the bushes is a saber-toothed tiger—and research has demonstrated that a severe tendency to jump to negative conclusions can be a hallmark of mental illness.[3] But for ordinary people, this tendency can still be problematic and needs to be avoided to the greatest extent possible.

No matter how long you've been together, or how many of life's ups and downs you've been through, you have to commit to hearing—*really hearing*—each communication as if you were meeting for the first time. Although this level of mindfulness may sound tedious, in time it becomes second nature and effortless. What could be more tedious than revisiting the same issues over and over again because you didn't make that small extra effort the *first* time?

The Hack

A big part of my ***Structured Dialog*** technique is the final step—asking the other party, "Is there anything else?" when they appear to be finished speaking. This is the point at which that last crucial bit of information may come out that changes the entire context of whatever has come before. Linguists have a saying, "You can never interrupt a German." This is because the structure of the German language often appends important parts of speech to the very end of the sentence. If one interrupts, one risks completely misunderstanding the speaker. This can be just as true of any difficult communication in which you don't take extra care to be certain you've gotten the *complete* message from the other party. We seldom speak in wholly complete thoughts; often we are still formulating our message as we go along. If you don't give a speaker an opportunity to reflect and provide any missing information, miscommunication is a frequent result.

Keep notes on each difficult or unsatisfying conversation you have, and in reviewing them, reflect upon whether you were consistent in asking this critical question—"Is there anything else you'd like to say?" If not, you must redouble your effort to include this in every dialogue until it becomes second nature.

James R. Fleckenstein

To effectively communicate, we must realize that we are all different in the way we perceive the world and use this understanding as a guide to our communication with others.
~ Tony Robbins

Your mindset is everything in your effort to understand and be understood. No two people perceive the world or experience it identically. Each of us is a unique individual, and each of us brings a unique perspective based on our long-term history (*e.g.*, upbringing, culture, race, life experiences, spiritual practices/orientation) and experience as well as our immediate circumstances (*e.g.*, stuck in traffic, kids acting up, health issues) to every interaction. Instead of struggling to ignore this reality and its consequences, one important skill in communicating is to accept difference and embrace it. By doing this, we dramatically improve our chances of achieving complete communication.

For example, our highly-developed and effective sense of sight depends in part upon the particular placement of our eyes; because each eye sees a slightly different picture, our brain is able to perceive depth and distance. Translate that reality into your communication with your partner. Because each of you *always* sees everything differently—to varying degrees—you jointly are better able to understand the reality of things. But this happens only if you don't approach the task with one hand held over your eye, figuratively speaking, through failing to appreciate and use your differing perspectives to gain a better understanding.

The Hack

Make it a point to learn to value your partner's different take on things. We are trained to try to value diversity of viewpoints in our commercial lives, yet we instinctively seem to shun this diversity in our personal and relational world. We expect perfect harmony, if not complete unanimity. When this expectation isn't met (as it cannot be), discord often ensues.

Begin to build a habit of not only *asking* for your partner's views, but also genuinely *appreciating* the additional insight their views provide. This isn't to say that you will (or should) always wholly agree, but the path to growth and a richer relationship lies in building a heartfelt appreciation for the differences between you, and how those differences contribute to, rather than detracting from, a more complete ability to communicate.

James R. Fleckenstein

Extremists think "communication" means agreeing with them.

~ Leo Rosten

I don't mean to characterize all couples as extremists, but I often find that complaints about communication in relationships really boil down to one or both parties feeling that they can't get to an agreement *that is favorable to their viewpoint.* They mistakenly believe that if they could just communicate better, the obvious superiority of their position would become clear to their partner! This delusion lies at the heart of many "communication" difficulties, and is something I often have to unravel. I see people who just keep repeating themselves, and in many cases "turning up the (emotional and actual) volume" of their communication. A variation of this is when people withdraw from communicating (often it is men who do this) because they can't get their partners to accept their viewpoint.

It's certainly true that better communication ultimately will lead to more agreement, but in a fair number of cases, that might just be an agreement to disagree. Even if that's true, it's vastly better to have a clear understanding than to be constantly arguing about the same issues over and over. Relationship researcher John

Gottman, in analyzing over three decades of research with couples, has concluded that *every* couple has at least 10 irreconcilable differences.[4] If you're aground on one of these, no amount of communicating is going to change things. Wisdom lies in using good communication skills to become aware that you're at an impasse, and then negotiating a way to live comfortably with your disagreement.

The Hack Take a few minutes and write down a list of up to 10 "irreconcilable differences" between you and your partner, the real hard sticking points in your relationship. If you have fewer than 10, good for you, but be sure you're not being lazy or fearful of writing things down. I'm not talking about little things like ice cream flavors or favorite colors, but rather real differences that may have sparked a genuine conflict between you that you haven't yet resolved, despite repeated efforts. Invite your partner to do the same privately and separately, then compare lists. If they're not pretty much identical, explore where they differ and why that might be.

The idea here is to develop a mutually agreed-upon list. Once you've done that, set the list aside for 60 days, then revisit it together. If you're still in agreement that these are the "sticking point" issues in your relationship, decide together which of them (or even *all* of them) will hereafter no longer be the subject of conflict between you. Essentially, these are the matters on which you mutually agree to disagree and to give up trying to change each other. Then stick to that agreement! It's ok to have an annual revisiting of the list to see if things have changed, but you have to agree in advance to that practice as well. You might be surprised at how much more harmonious your relationship becomes when you take these off the table! (See "Irreconcilable Differences" Worksheet, page 207)

Every relationship has its problems. But if you're not willing to honestly express how you feel, how can you ever expect things to get better?

~ **Stephan Labossiere**

One of the biggest obstacles to communication is our socially-conditioned fear of honesty and of confrontation. We would often rather attempt to avoid addressing a problem until it simply becomes too big to ignore. At that point, the stakes have become so high that reasoned discussion becomes very difficult. As the saying goes, "denial is not just a river in Egypt." We have a perfect right to our own feelings. We have an equal responsibility for both managing them appropriately and expressing them thoughtfully. Both of these statements are equally true for our partners.

One of the most important gifts we can give each other in a relationship is the gift of honesty and forthrightness. Using what I say in this book, and especially if you gain familiarity with my techniques of **Safe Space** and **Structured Dialog**, you can both feel safe in being honest, and have the skills to state your positions clearly and with mutual understanding. Overcoming the temporary discomfort in getting your feelings and needs out on the table is essential to

James R. Fleckenstein

building a healthy and nourishing relationship for the long run.

The Hack Think about any "sticking point" issues you feel you have in your relationship. (The previous hack may help with this, but here I'm talking mostly about issues that *haven't* yet surfaced.) Have you actually *had* a conversation with your partner about them? Was it recently? If you answer "no" to either of these questions, I invite you to select one of these concerns and make it a point to begin a conversation with your partner about it. Don't cop out by telling yourself, "Oh, it's really not that important." If that's true, then it's even better as practice because the stakes won't be so high for you. Commit to doing this in the next two weeks. After the conversation, reflect on how it went. Then invite your partner to do the same with any issues they have been harboring without raising. (See "Surfacing the Issue" Worksheet, page 208)

James R. Fleckenstein

CHAPTER 3
The Third Pillar – *Mindful Reason*

———————— 🖤 ————————

Bringing mindfulness to processing everything you hear is an essential practice. Without it, you remain captive to emotional forces that can utterly undo you and your relationship. Engaging the power of your conscious mind, and taking full personal responsibility for your thoughts and actions, is the key to putting you in control of every situation.

Mindful Reason is my adaptation of the pioneering work of Albert Ellis in combination with the recent application of timeless principles of mindfulness. Ellis created *Rational Emotive Behavioral Therapy*, the basis for much of the entire field of cognitive behavioral therapy. His contribution led to his peers voting him the second most influential psychologist of the 20th century, outscoring even Sigmund Freud!

Where it fits
Once you have set the stage for effective communication, you have to accept responsibility for what you do with the

information you receive. **Mindful Reason** is the tool you can use to achieve that. For example, it comes in very handy when:

- You've been told something you find problematic at first blush
- You have something to say that you believe your partner may find problematic
- Your self-talk becomes problematic and is creating friction in your life and/or your relationship

By practicing **Mindful Reason**, you naturally increase your **Differentiation of Self**, which in turn leads to better relationships.

How it works

Ellis laid out a simple progression of how we cognitively process experiences. He called it the ABCDE model.[1] A is an *Activating Event*— something tangible that can be objectively observed by anyone. C is your emotional *Consequence*, or reaction to that event. The common simplistic view is that A *causes* C; something happens, and you have a reaction as a result. Ellis' brilliant contribution was to note that there is an intervening step—B—which represents your *Beliefs* about the event. These beliefs color and to some extent dictate your reaction. You react as you do because your internal beliefs, values, and judgments tell you that this is how you *should* react. But what if you're unhappy or troubled by your reaction? What if it brings you suffering, hardship, and emotional pain? Ellis correctly points out that, while you have no godlike control over *events*, you have complete control over your *beliefs*.

If you find that you want to alter the emotional outcomes of acting on your beliefs as they exist, you must *Dispute*—the D step in the model— these beliefs that are the *real* cause of your emotional pain. Many of our beliefs are what Ellis terms "irrational." They are based on demonstrably false assumptions, often "all-or-nothing" propositions, or similarly problematic premises. By examining these irrational beliefs and disputing their validity with our power of reason we can change our emotional consequences.

Some examples of irrational beliefs that can get in the way of our peace of mind include:

- Demandingness—that events absolutely *should* and *must* go in the way I find acceptable
- Inflexibility/rigidity—that there is only *one* right way for events to occur and only *one* truly valid and correct outcome
- Awfulizing/catastrophizing—if events somehow fail to occur in the manner I desire and expect, that is truly *awful* and a great catastrophe
- "I-can't-stand-it-itis"—if events are catastrophic and do not occur in the manner I desire and expect, I simply can't stand it! I deserve better, and this *should not* happen!

- Personalizing—This *always* happens to me, and *only* to me! Everyone else seems to be doing just fine and doesn't have to deal with these kinds of terrible events

Obviously, these are exaggerated for effect, but we often fall victim to less extreme versions of this kind of thinking. If we don't use mindfulness to step back and notice when this happens, we are powerless to bring our calmer, rational mind to bear and successfully dispute these damaging ways of looking at the world. The E in Ellis' model stands for *New Effect*—the more rational, less painful and more accurate beliefs that we adopt as a result of disputing the crippling irrational beliefs.

This only scratches the surface—there's a lot more to Ellis' approach, and I've melded it in with contemporary research and practice around mindfulness to create my ***Mindful Reason*** Pillar.

LOVE THAT WORKS

James R. Fleckenstein

How people treat you is their karma; how you react is yours.
~ Wayne Dyer

The only person you can really control in this life is yourself. Much of the struggle in relationships is rooted in a desire to change or control your partner. *Please give that up!* Many arguments are created because of our reactivity. If you step back and take personal responsibility for your reactions to what you hear, you are often able to avoid the trap of escalating a conversation into a conflict. It is often not the actuality of what is being communicated, but our *interpretation* of it that engenders conflict. Accept that you're not going to rewrite your partner's history. You can't change the past. You do, however, have unlimited power over what you *choose* to do in the present. You're responsible for yourself, and *only* yourself, in emotional and practical terms.

If you've learned to set the stage for clear communication by co-creating **Safe Space**, and you've been diligent in making sure you seek first to understand, then to be understood by using **Structured Dialog**, now is the time to process what you're hearing in an orderly manner using my **Mindful Reason** technique.

A consistent theme throughout this book is the concept of personal re-empowerment, expressed in a variety of ways. I'm asking you to step up, take personal responsibility for what you *can* control, and stop sweating the things you *can't* control – the unchangeable past, the thoughts and reactions of others, the weather, and so on. Every situation you encounter offers you a choice in how you react. The choices you make determine whether you experience peace and some degree of happiness in life – even in the face of adversity – or instead find yourself consistently anxious, frustrated, angry, or bitter. These choices obviously have enormous impact on your relationships, your partner, and the satisfaction you feel within your relationship.

The Hack

One of the cornerstones of *Affirmative Intimacy*™ is *Mindful Reason*, developed from Albert Ellis' Rational Emotive Behavioral Therapy. In effect, you control every situation life throws at you by doing the only thing you truly can—controlling *yourself*. Next time any situation in life is "getting your goat"—a traffic jam, a rude service provider, a long hold on the phone—try stepping back mentally and then consciously deciding how you *want* to react. Is the situation really worth getting upset about? Can you do *anything* to change it? If not, then why not change your reaction?

Once you've gained some practice with this approach, try applying this skill to a situation with your partner that threatens to irritate you or provoke a problematic reaction from you. Does it help? This is a skill that must be practiced to become ingrained. You might want to keep notes of situations where you've either successfully or unsuccessfully tried to apply this skill. This can serve as a record of your progress and a guide to areas of opportunity for your efforts.

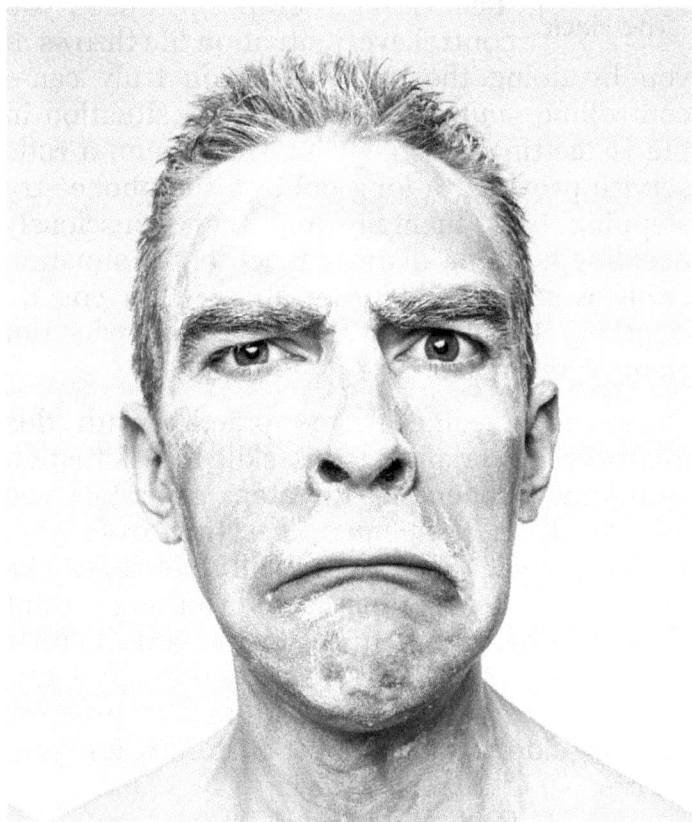

You're only responsible for being honest, not for someone else's reaction to your honesty.
~ Kelli Jae Baeli

This is the mirror image of the previous quote. Just as you are only able to control yourself when receiving information, you are likewise *not responsible* for how your partner chooses to process information you share. That is solely and completely up to them. The temptation to try to manage your partner's reactions by "spinning" your information is great. You *must* resist. To do otherwise is both dishonest and counterproductive. While you may delay the consequences of honesty for a while, inevitably the truth will out and the consequences will be far worse when you add deception and disempowerment to the mix. You have to give your partner the opportunity to be who they are and react as they will. You may not like that, but if you expect that freedom for yourself—and you should—there's no avoiding the responsibility to extend it to your partner.

The idea here is to step back from trying to shape or control your partner's reaction and just accept it. They are going to do and be what seems best to them in the moment, but you can't and shouldn't internalize that in any way. *Of course, you have no obligation to be*

passive in the face of emotional or physical abuse of any kind! Should this occur, you have a right and obligation to remove yourself from the situation immediately. But absent abuse, your role is to observe, process, and work to continue the dialogue as honestly and lovingly as you possibly can.

The Hack

The next time you find yourself accepting responsibility for the feelings of others, stop and reassess. You are always responsible for your actions, but not for the feelings others adopt. Please accept this as your mantra—"Nothing I do ever *makes* anybody feel anything they don't *choose* to feel. Nothing anybody else does ever *makes* me feel anything I don't *choose* to feel." Just as you are not free to offload responsibility for your feelings onto others, you must stand resolute against others offloading their feelings onto you. You have a duty to be respectfully honest and forthright; you have no duty to manage others' reactions. Always strive to act carefully and with consideration, but, having acted, abide the outcome with integrity and equanimity.

James R. Fleckenstein

When you say or do anything to please, get, keep, influence, or control anyone or anything, fear is the cause and pain is the result.

~ **Byron Katie**

You are always responsible for yourself. You are never *responsible*, in the strictest sense, for anybody else. We generally are trained from childhood to "dance the dance" of manipulation, whether of parents, siblings, teachers, or others important to us. We then carry those bad habits of mind right through the dating and courtship process and into our relationships. But Katie is absolutely right! Fear *is* the cause and pain *is* the inevitable result. Pause a moment and let that sink in. We "spin" the truth because we are afraid of the consequences of truth-telling. *What* we're afraid of is that we couldn't successfully manage those consequences. So, we spin, we lie, we evade, wheedle, cajole, and demand—all in hope of avoiding confronting the childhood fears that were instilled in us when we were truly helpless and powerless children, largely at the mercy of the adults charged with our care. Is this *really* who you want to be, now that you are an adult? The tactics appropriate to children are not going to bring satisfaction and true peace of mind to an adult.

By applying the principles of the **Mindful Reason** technique, you can reclaim your true resilience and exercise your power as an adult to weather the consequences of honesty. You'll also reap the benefits of avoiding the needless suffering your fears impose upon you, and the emotional trauma that always follows the discovery of your dishonesty and manipulation.

The Hack

The next time you're tempted to "spin" a statement to evade the imagined consequences of being forthright, catch yourself. Are you accepting responsibility for the reactions and internal processes of others? Why? What do you need to do to break this destructive habit?

Consider exactly what it is you're afraid of happening or not happening if you don't spin your remark. Consciously weigh the real-world consequences of truthfulness using your logical, adult mind. Then try to state your truth considerately, tactfully, but without spin or attempted manipulation. Stop and relish the different, positive feeling you enjoy when you act with authenticity.

James R. Fleckenstein

The only real security is not in owning or possessing, not in demanding or expecting, not in hoping, even. Security in a relationship lies neither in looking back to what it was, nor forward to what it might be, but living in the present and accepting it as it is now.

~ Anne Morrow Lindbergh

You can only live in the present. Your relationship only exists in the present. It is an ever-evolving process, but the outcome of that evolution is essentially unknowable. Nevertheless, we too often find ourselves consumed by things that have happened in the past, wrongs we believe have been done to us, shortcomings that we have allowed to bring us pain, and the like. In the same vein, too many of us look constantly to the future, vividly imagining that things will get better "if only." Both types of thinking are nothing more than mental and emotional quicksand. By ignoring the simple reality that today is all we have, we deny or defer responsibility for taking actions which may stretch us, or make us uncomfortable.

Once again, to follow this wise counsel is not to abandon any aspirations toward improvement in your relationship. Rather, it is to realize that the only real hope you have of achieving that improvement is by gracefully accepting the way things are *today*. From that grounded vantage point, you can begin doing the work *today* that will bring the future results you desire. *Doing*, not dreaming or demanding or expecting, will accomplish all that can be done to give you security.

The Hack

Work to avoid "if only" thinking. Any time you find yourself tempted to revisit the past or get lost in future dreaming, try to refocus your thinking and your emotional energy on what's happening *now*. If you have a concern, ask yourself, "What can I do about that *right now*?" That's not to say you're going to *solve* the problem right now; some things take time, even years, to resolve completely. But the essence here is to do something now—however small—to begin that process, rather than simply worrying over it and letting your anxiety build needlessly.

Write a list of the top three concerns you have in your relationship today. Then, in a second column next to each, write three things that you could do *within the next week* to improve those concerns. These steps may be as simple as challenging your mental reaction to the problem, or as complex as enlisting your partner in a multi-step process to improve matters over time. The essence, though, is to identify things you can do *right now*. Success breeds success, and once you've begun to see results from developing this "bias for action" mindset, you'll wonder why you didn't do this before! (See "Taking Action Now" Worksheet, page 209)

James R. Fleckenstein

Begin challenging your own assumptions. Your assumptions are your windows on the world. Scrub them off every once in awhile, or the light won't come in.
~ **Alan Alda**

We are all victims of our assumptions. We assume peoples' motivations, their thoughts, or their beliefs. Yet we rarely, if ever, seek to validate our assumptions. Worse still, we let those untested and possibly erroneous assumptions control our actions and our thoughts about ourselves. We too often limit ourselves because we assume things that may be completely false. We give ourselves limiting and negative self-messages that hold us back from the growth and happiness we seek.

With *Mindful Reason* techniques, we can challenge our limiting assumptions about ourselves and others. We can also contend more easily with life's inevitable challenges by stripping away the self-created fears we hold based on these unexamined assumptions. We need certain basic assumptions to get through our day-to-day existence, but whenever you feel yourself distressed, angry, or frustrated, stop and question your assumptions about what's going on.

You are probably familiar with the vulgar saying about assuming. If you consistently find yourself distressed by a situation, a person's actions, or how you feel you're being treated, you'll need to build up an ability to step back and see what assumptions you're making about the situation and how they might be coloring your reaction in inappropriate and harmful ways. As I've noted, there are many times when we don't have the complete story. Our overactive imaginations are only too ready to "fill in the blanks" with "information" that may be completely divorced from reality. It's certainly convenient to operate this way, and in some things it really doesn't matter. But in others, it can be a real problem.

The Hack

Whenever you find yourself tempted to act in the absence of reasonably complete knowledge, based solely on an assumption, cultivate the ability to stop and "clean the windows." Ask yourself, "Do I really know *all* that I need to before I say/do/believe this, or am I operating on the basis of what I *assume* to be so?" If you find yourself frequently tempted to act based on assumptions, work to reground yourself in the practice of looking for the facts before acting, even if it takes more time and effort to do so. Taking this extra time up front will save you hours (possibly years) of grief and embarrassment down the road.

James R. Fleckenstein

Learning that you can't control the other person's reaction, and that it can be destructive to try, can be incredibly liberating. It not only gives the other person the space to react however they need to, but also takes a huge amount of pressure off you. You will learn things about yourself based on their reaction, but if you are prepared to learn, you'll feel free from the desperate need for their reaction to go one certain way.

~ Douglas Stone

This is a crucial insight. Trying to control others is almost always destructive as well as futile in most cases! Stone is correct that giving up your need/desire to control what the other person is thinking/feeling is a tremendously freeing experience. Attempting control is just another form of taking personal responsibility for the inner workings of others, and it nearly always brings a burden of frustration and anxiety.

With techniques like ***Mindful Reason***, you can accept whatever reaction you get with equanimity, because you can separate what you hear from who you are, and likewise, separate what the other person says or feels from who *they* are. As Stone points out, every interaction is a learning and growth opportunity for both of you! Gratefully accept it as such.

The Hack

Stone's message here is simple. Next time you find yourself imagining you can control someone's reaction to a situation, or *wanting* to, step back and ask yourself why it's so important that they react in a certain way? What are the real stakes? What have you come to believe their reaction means about you? *Why* do you believe that? Does that belief serve you, or shackle you?

Practice taking that step back at every opportunity, and gradually begin to wean yourself off the compulsion to try to control others.

Mindfulness helps us freeze the frame so that we can become aware of our sensations and experiences as they are, without the distorting coloration of socially conditioned responses or habitual reactions.

~ Henepola Gunaratana

I love how Gunaratana nails this! We all can and do fall victim to "socially conditioned responses" and "habitual reactions." This is personally disempowering. You're trading away your human right to think for yourself and experience everything in life on your own terms. I encounter this with the people I've worked with when I challenge their thinking about situations. They often respond with variations on "Well, *anybody* would feel that way!" or "That's what I'm *supposed* to feel!" That's when I have to step in and gently help pry their thinking out of the mental rut of these socially-conditioned responses that may be getting in the way of their progress.

By practicing **Mindful Reason**, you become able to step back from knee-jerk reactions and step toward better behavior that enhances your personal empowerment and sense of inner peace. You are freed to evaluate the situation and circumstance in a clear-headed manner, and consciously choose the most appropriate course of action. This practice takes cultivation and repetition, like any change in your approach to life, but the dividends it pays are priceless!

The Hack Every time you find yourself in an interaction that triggers your fears and therefore causes you to default to thoughts or responses that may not be wholly your own, work to develop the ability to bring your conscious mind to bear. By doing this, you accomplish the miraculous task of slowing down time and giving yourself the opportunity to make a considered choice about what you're feeling and how you *want* to act. Like any "mental muscle," this ability takes exercise to grow stronger.

I recommend you keep a journal for a few months in which you write down some notes about challenging situations you encounter and how you choose to react to them. Hopefully over time you will gain an increasing ability to step back from impulsive thoughts and reactions. Whenever you lapse from your discipline, review the journal to remind yourself that you *can* do this, and reflect upon how much better you felt when you were in control.

James R. Fleckenstein

When we direct our thoughts properly, we can control our emotions.

~ W. Clement Stone

Seriously, who among us truly relishes being captive to our emotional demons? Yet society and our own intellectual laziness conspire to forge chains that take conscious effort first even to *see*, and then to break. These habitual chains to our emotional reactions weigh us down, impede our ability to have rich and fulfilling relationships, and enslave us to the opinions of others. Because we somewhere internalized a belief that *X* is how we "should" feel or react in a given situation, we unthinkingly do so, whether *X* actually benefits us or not, or advances our growth and inner peace. Like the "Dark Side of the Force," this practice is "quicker, easier, more seductive" but no less damaging to our emotional well-being and maturity.

As I noted above, when confronted, we frequently retreat to the logical fallacy known as the "appeal to common practice," *e.g.,* "well, *anybody* would feel exactly the same as I do in this situation." Aside from being utterly unprovable, it cedes all responsibility for your own thoughts and actions. Is this *really* what you want to do? I suggest you should not. The real beauty of my suggested approach lies not in stripping our lives from the vitality that passion brings—we are not meant to be coldly rational, passionless beings—but rather puts us *in control* of our passions. Then we can direct our passion in positive ways to achieve our life and relationship goals.

The Hack

Once again, **Mindful Reason** calls on us to pause, step back and make a conscious choice regarding how we react. This is simple, but not easy. Nevertheless, if you desire the inner peace and emotional stability this approach offers, begin working on it *today*.

When you find yourself justifying your irrational thoughts on the basis of the common practice fallacy, I invite you to stop and reflect upon whether you want to be "just another sheep" or a person who is in control of their own feelings and behaviors. If the latter, then decide the best course of action for you at this time, and act upon it. When the moment is past, reflect upon how you felt. Was it not better, calmer, more in control?

James R. Fleckenstein

Every day we have plenty of opportunities to get angry, stressed or offended. But what you're doing when you indulge these negative emotions is giving something outside yourself power over your happiness.

~ **Joel Osteen**

Is this ever true! We unthinkingly let ourselves react to external events and other people, never realizing that by doing so, we totally disempower ourselves. We cede control of ourselves to these external forces. We let events and people "make" us feel angry, sad, frustrated, and so on. But this is a fallacy. Nobody and nothing can ever "make" us feel anything we don't *choose* to feel. History is rife with examples of people who survived great hardship, deprivation, enslavement, even physical and mental torture, because they somehow understood and called upon the strength that comes from inner conviction.[2] How much smaller are your day-to-day stresses?

Please understand, I'm not talking about isolating yourself from your humanity! Our human emotions are an essential part of who we are. It's perfectly natural to respond emotionally to outside events. But—and this is crucial— beyond that initial reaction, anything that follows is entirely within our control. We *choose* to indulge and incorporate the emotional reaction beyond the split-second initial experience. If the emotion is positive and beneficial, we can choose to relish and sustain it. If it is harmful, stressful, or negative, we can choose to step back and remove its sting. By applying techniques like **Mindful Reason** to these stressful situations we all encounter in life, we can consciously choose to be happier, more fulfilled, and more at peace. Trust me—you will have better, happier, and more joyful relationships as well!

The Hack

The theme of this chapter is **Mindful Reason**, my technique for managing your reactivity. As with the other quotations, what Osteen is saying calls upon each of us to stop disempowering ourselves by surrendering our emotional autonomy. In the modern world, very few of us are granted a life without many opportunities for anger, irritation, disappointment, or stress. What can make a difference is how we choose to manage those opportunities.

Begin today to see these opportunities in your daily life as tools for your personal growth; blessings rather than irritants. When someone cuts you off in traffic, when someone is rude to you in a line, when a co-worker fails to meet their responsibilities, when your children are being singularly ill-behaved—try to treat these as learning experiences. Begin re-educating yourself to take control of your own emotions and re-empower yourself. Once you've mastered these simpler daily tasks, you'll be better prepared to take on the bigger challenges you face in relationship—disagreements about money, child rearing, in-laws, or sex—and re-establish your peace and tranquility when faced with potentially problematic happenings.

James R. Fleckenstein

CHAPTER 4
The Fourth Pillar – *Differentiation of Self*
———————— 💗 ————————

Being your authentic self (and expecting the same of your partner) is the key to a healthy and fulfilling relationship.

With respect to retaining personal responsibility and accountability while in relationship, I studied the work of psychiatrist Murray Bowen. Bowen developed his Family Systems Theory through decades of painstaking research. Psychologist David Schnarch then developed a method for using Bowen's principles in couples therapy. Bowen and Schnarch identified "differentiation of self" as critical to sustainable relationships. I felt that Albert Ellis' REBT—the inspiration for my *Mindful Reason* Pillar—was a perfect tool for improving one's differentiation of self. Melding Bowen's and Schnarch's insights with Ellis' discoveries gave me much of the basis for the *Differentiation of Self* Pillar of *Affirmative Intimacy*™.

Theologian Thomas F. Fischer, writing for pastors, defined differentiation of self as, "...a term used to describe one whose emotional process is no longer ultimately dependent on anything other than themselves. They are able to live and function on their own without undue anxiety or over-dependence on others. They are self-sufficient. Their sense of worth is not dependent on external relationships, circumstances or occurrences."[1] I think this is as good a working definition as I've seen.

The lack of differentiation of self shows up in intimate relationships as "emotional fusion" which can mean being *too* close to your partner and *too* sensitive to the emotional anxiety present in the relationship, *or* by "emotional cutoff," which is deliberate distancing within the relationship to avoid the anxiety. Neither is helpful. There is a robust body of research that demonstrates that the more differentiated the partners in a relationship are, the happier and more satisfying the relationship is perceived to be.[2, 3, 4, 5]

Where it fits
Once you gain the skills of co-creating **Safe Space**, using **Structured Dialog**, and viewing issues through the lens of **Mindful Reason**, your level of **Differentiation of Self** will certainly grow. To maximize that growth, I encourage you to focus specifically on applying these other tools consistently in your journey toward becoming a more independent, yet still fully present, participant in your relationship.

How it works
As noted above, the well-differentiated person is equipped to "stand on their own two feet" emotionally. They have moved beyond

reflexively reacting to the others around them and allowing themselves to be overwhelmed and subdued by the anxiety often present in relationships. They have moved beyond any dependent and self-negating role they may have internalized from their family of origin, and have positioned themselves to be a fully functioning adult. Paradoxically, it is this very independence and freedom from excessive reactivity to the emotions of others that makes the well-differentiated person an attractive and supportive partner. I tend to convey the sense of this to the people I've worked with by means of the metaphor, "put on your own oxygen mask before assisting others."

A deep dive into the workings of increasing one's differentiation of self is beyond the scope of this work, but I am always ready to help if you find this concept valuable.

James R. Fleckenstein

Once the realization is accepted that even between the closest human beings infinite distances continue, a wonderful living side by side can grow, if they succeed in loving the distance between them which makes it possible for each to see the other whole against the sky.

~ Rainer Maria Rilke

The concept of romantic love in Western culture, shaped by medieval troubadours, builds on the neurotransmitter-fueled infatuation of "falling in love" to create a picture of inseparable lovers. This is as unhealthy as it is unsustainable. Rilke correctly sees that this illusion denies us the opportunity to appreciate, and be appreciated by, our beloved as a complete and independent person. This same pernicious belief system—that our partner is supposed to be *everything* for us—sets us up for jealousy, insecurity, fear, bitterness and a host of other negatives that are actually easily avoidable.

Once the original "falling in love" neurochemical rush wears off—and it almost always does—Rilke's approach sets us up for a long and happy partnership, rather than sending us chasing off in search of a *new* "one true love." Becoming at peace with the healthy distance between you, rather than fretting too much that you're "growing apart," is an important step toward maturity. Living together contentedly, supportively, and lovingly "side-by-side" is the essence of my technique for achieving *Differentiation of Self*.

The Hack The "togetherness ethos" imposed by Western culture is suffocating. If you haven't done so up to now, start to become healthier by trying to cultivate a new hobby or significant interest that your partner *doesn't* share. Don't let your new enthusiasm make it an overwhelming time sink, or budget-buster—doing that will create new and thorny challenges to confront! *Don't* try to involve your partner. If this new interest helps you to build a new friendship network—with individuals of *both* genders—even better! It is probably a good idea to have a preliminary conversation with your partner about this, and why you're doing it. Resist any attempt by your partner to make it about *them*. Hopefully by now you have some of the skills I've introduced here to assist you with this.

The concept is to begin to recreate the individual and separate person your partner fell in love with—*before* they fell in love with you. Each of you deserves to have friends, activities and interests that are *yours alone*—as a discrete individual. Doing so will both increase your own self-esteem and sense of personal autonomy and also afford you and your partner opportunities to see each other as separate, complete human beings. The stifling cloak of couplehood gets really itchy after a while, so it's perfectly fine to leave it in the closet periodically! Familiarity may not breed contempt, but *individuality* definitely breeds interest and attractiveness!

James R. Fleckenstein

The beginning of love is to let those we love be perfectly themselves, and not to twist them to fit our own image. Otherwise we love only the reflection of ourselves we find in them.
~ **Thomas Merton**

Many of us have a hard time letting our partners be perfectly themselves. A quotation often attributed to Albert Einstein reads, "Men marry women with the hope they will never change. Women marry men with the hope they will change. Invariably they are both disappointed." This doesn't seem to keep many of us in relationships from trying to change our partners in fundamental ways, and usually in the direction of being more like ourselves. This is a mistake, not to mention often futile and a source of great strife. At the root of these efforts is often a deep sense of insecurity and more than a little fear. In terms of the guiding theories about *Differentiation of Self*, this effort to enforce conformity at any cost is a manifestation of a drive for emotional fusion, which Bowen defines as "where individual choices are set aside in service of achieving harmony in the system." This is rarely healthy. If the depth and quality of our love for each other is measured only by the degree to which we are alike, it is *never* healthy.

None of this is to say that we should not freely and tactfully share our views with each other, and encourage personal growth. However, we must cultivate the ability to accept our partners *as they are*, not as we would wish them to be, and demand the same for ourselves.

The Hack Like so many other action steps, this one involves catching yourself in the act, and consciously deciding to act differently. Stop trying to shape your partner, or make them a clone of you. Learn to value your differences, and see them as complementary rather than competitive or a source for concern. This extends with equal (if not greater) force to matters in which you don't particularly appreciate your partner's taste or preferences. Barring conduct which is objectively harmful to others or legally proscribed, we are not in relationship to be each other's parents, guardians, censors, or drill instructors! Give each other the space to be full adults, and work hard to avoid seeking to impose your tastes or values onto your partner.

Try writing a list of five significant characteristics of your partner that you most wish you could change. Were these characteristics apparent, even if only faintly visible, when your relationship began, or did they only become apparent after time? Have you discussed them with your partner? How do you think your relationship would be different if you could magically change these aspects of your partner? Would it truly be better, and if so, why? Would changing these characteristics make your partner behave/think/react more like you? Is that necessarily a good thing, and why?

Look for patterns in your thinking that reflect a desire to "reform" your partner to make them more like you and repress or eliminate their individuality strictly for the sake of your own comfort or convenience. (See "Changing Your Partner" Worksheet, page 210)

James R. Fleckenstein

But let there be spaces in your togetherness and let the winds of the heavens dance between you. Love one another but make not a bond of love: let it rather be a moving sea between the shores of your souls.

~ Khalil Gibran

Gibran's poetic imagery is compelling to me. Too often love becomes a bond, a fetter, a source of expectations and pain rather than of joy. This stems in part from the misguided conception of a healthy loving relationship as one of complete unity rather than as a cooperative partnership between two emotionally whole and separate individuals. When we lose sight of that, we find ourselves shackled by our love, rather than empowered by it. We expect our partner to be our sole source of sexual gratification, economic and social support, emotional confidant and nurturer, best friend, activity partner of last resort, etc. Through a cultural accident of the last 70-100 years, we have gradually demolished the roles played by other people and institutions outside our nuclear family and loaded them onto the backs of our partners. Research demonstrates conclusively that when couples marry or enter cohabitation, friendship and kinship ties often suffer. [6, 7, 8]

Maintaining a healthy distance between you makes it possible to revel in the togetherness you choose to create for yourselves. It's paradoxical, but proven by both science and folk wisdom, that trying to get and stay too close to your partner ends up creating not harmony, but discord. *Differentiation of Self* is an ideal to strive for. It lets you be an emotionally whole person while maintaining an important relationship. I believe that by employing techniques discussed here and embodied in the first three Pillars of my *Affirmative Intimacy*™. approach, the fourth Pillar—*Differentiation of Self*—becomes achievable.

The Hack

Gibran puts poetically what we know in our hearts to be true. Begin trying to build a little healthy space into your relationship. Wherever you've fallen into an unconscious habit of "automatic togetherness," whether at mealtimes, watching TV, or doing other routine things together without consciously thinking about it, step back and *think about it*! Consciously plan time apart. Start small if you need to, then work up to more significant separations from time to time. A generation or two ago, this kind of separation for at least a weekend at a time was much more common—hunting trips, conventions, etc. Now we have replaced that with enforced togetherness such that an expressed desire for a weekend apart engenders suspicion rather than encouragement!

We cannot fully appreciate the value of being together without ever being apart. Not merely because life circumstances force separation—*e.g.,* you work at different places—but because we have consciously *chosen* to be apart for a time, and then have *chosen* to be together again. You'll be surprised at the positive feelings these "mini-reunions" will generate! Some research even demonstrates that they will often lead to positive sparks in the bedroom![9,10,11]

James R. Fleckenstein

The concept of differentiation has to do with self and not with others. Differentiation deals with working on one's own self, with controlling self, with becoming a more responsible person, and permitting others to be themselves.

~ **Murray Bowen**

Bowen has zeroed in on the most important aspect of his theory here. ***Differentiation of Self*** is essentially a completely self-contained process. It consists of doing the work to become your own person, whole, intact, fully worthy of love and perfectly capable of participating in a healthy loving relationship. Just as importantly, it calls us to give up on our "projects" of trying to change others in our lives.

To be fully ourselves, we must accept the right and responsibility of others close to us to be themselves as they are, not as we would prefer them to be; or worse still, *need* them to be. Our culture encourages and endorses unhealthy emotional fusion between partners; it takes courage and conscious effort to rise above this pressure. We must seek to become an independent person *in a relationship*, rather than a person *dependent upon* a relationship.

> **The Hack**
>
> Take a few moments to reflect upon your attitudes about your relationship and write down what you find. If you weren't in this relationship, how would you feel? How would your life be different? What would you miss the most about being in this relationship? Your answers will clarify the degree to which you're depending on your relationship—or your partner—to "complete" you. Bowen invites us to work on our own completion and abandon attempts to mold our partners to fill in any "missing parts" of our personality.
>
> Begin today by thinking about aspects of your personality you rely upon your partner or your relationship to "complete" or compensate for. Then develop a plan to begin building your ability to handle these matters on your own, and stick to it! Some ideas to get your thinking started: if you are uncomfortable dealing with social arrangements and so always rely on your partner to handle them, begin gradually stretching yourself to become more involved; if you "just can't figure out finances," commit to learning more about the ins and outs of managing money and start taking an active and interested role in household finance matters. These are extremely simple ideas for weaning

yourself away from over-relying on your partner to let you off the hook, but you get the idea.

I don't mean abandoning the practical division of labor in your relationship—we all have strengths, weaknesses, and preferences—but rather I am encouraging you to make conscious choices rather than defaulting to roles that may have been assigned to you in your family of origin, but which now represent growth opportunities for your development.

James R. Fleckenstein

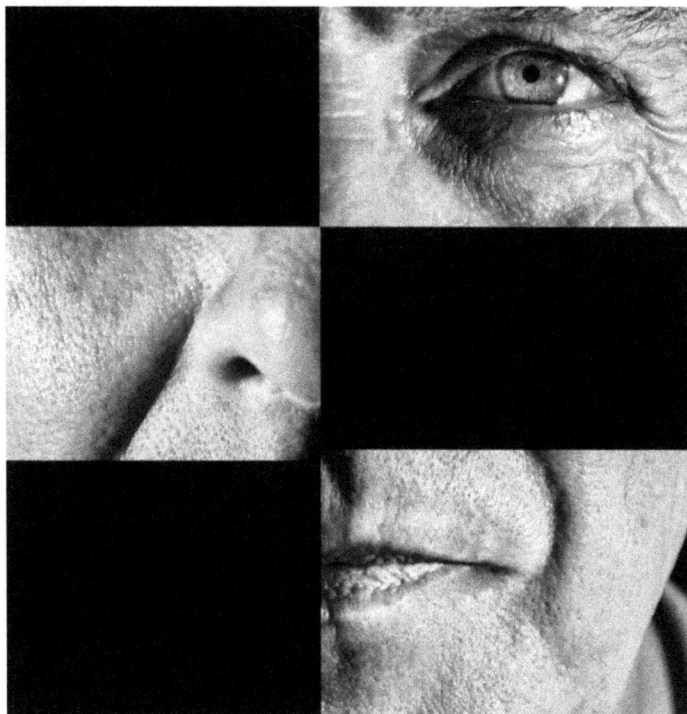

No partner in a love relationship... should feel that he has to give up an essential part of himself to make it viable.

~ **May Sarton**

Western culture generally and Christian thought/doctrine in particular have been heavily influenced by unhealthy aspects of Greek Stoicism (not all Stoicism is harmful—I endorse a fair amount of it myself!) that *over*-emphasize the nobility of sacrifice. We are taught to measure the value of things, people, and relationships not by their intrinsic worth, but rather by the degree to which we are willing to sacrifice for them. Apologists assert that this sacrifice should be joyful, and that failing to embrace it connotes selfishness and immaturity. To be blunt in the style of my own inspirator, Albert Ellis, this is pure hogwash!

I do believe that we should be willing to *compromise* with our partners and with life's "curveballs;" true selfishness and rigidity are *not* admirable. But as Sarton correctly points out, healthy people have healthy boundaries around what they are willing to compromise on, and what they are not. The six deadliest words in any relationship are "If you *really* loved me, you'd..." The instant they are spoken, it's time to run, not walk, for the exit!

You must insist on your absolute right to be and to retain your essential self, whole and intact, within your relationship. If you encounter any expectation that you sacrifice any aspect of your essential self to preserve the relationship, you should, of course, discuss *compromises* that might work, using skills like those I teach—**Safe Space**, **Structured Dialog**, and **Mindful Reason**. But in the end, you have a duty to yourself *and* to your partner to hold the line at making any sacrificial gestures that erode your ability to be a complete and independent person within the relationship. The hard truth is that it is better for you both that the relationship end or change than that you both become unhealthily enmeshed through misguided sacrifices of your essential personhood.

The Hack

Take some time to reflect upon your relationship, and the "choices" that you believe it has imposed on you. What have you been expected/coerced into "sacrificing for the sake of the relationship"? How much discomfort do you feel because of the lack of these practices, beliefs, or attitudes? Genuinely take the time to drill down to your real feelings; for the moment, forget about socially-imposed expectations. Make a list of the two or three most significant items, ones that really feel like you gave up a key aspect of your pre-relationship self. Then, put the shoe on the other foot. What have *you* expected your partner to sacrifice for the privilege of being in relationship with you? You should schedule a time to discuss these sacrifices with your partner, if possible using the tools of **Safe Space**, **Structured Dialog**, and **Mindful Reason**. The object is to work toward agreement to restore as many as possible of those things you've given up that represent real and painful losses for you and/or your partner. (See "(Un)Essential Sacrifices" Worksheet, page 211)

There are days when you need someone who just wants to be your sunshine and not the air you breathe.

~ **Robert Brault**

Brault captures an essential distinction here (though I'd quibble with Brault in that this should not be an occasional situation, but rather a permanent one). We should always hope to be the sunshine in each other's lives. But wanting to be the very air that you breathe? Something essential to your very survival? That seems just a bit unhealthy, no? Yet, undifferentiated couples fall into this trap all the time. We build a single interdependent "thing" that exists only by being conjoined in manifestly unhealthy ways. Unfortunately, many well-meaning helping professionals actually *foster* this problematic belief. Some go so far as to characterize "the relationship" as their client, rather than the people within it, and then work diligently "in the best interests of the relationship." Think about that for a minute; would you be happy with an attorney that you're consulting on a contract dispute who blithely informed you that she considered *the contract* her real client?

A truly healthy relationship exists between two whole, separate and complementary individuals who support and assist each other while maintaining their personal integrity and individuality. Both seek to grow and to develop their own personhood, and to *enable* the other to do the same. Each accepts that responsibility for themselves freely, and neither accepts nor desires to take on responsibility for implementing the other's growth or development.

The Hack Think about a time when you felt like your partner was getting "too close" or was expecting you to move in perfect lockstep with him/her. How did that feel? Was it an affirming and positive feeling, or did it feel suffocating to you? Healthy relationships happen when each partner gives the other sufficient space. When you find yourself feeling overwhelmed with closeness, commit to stepping back and sharing your feelings with your partner about why that doesn't work well for you. If you find yourself tempted to fasten onto your partner in unhealthy ways, especially when you're experiencing challenges or doubts, try to recognize this and wean yourself away from this pattern of behavior.

Differentiation is your ability to maintain your sense of self when you are emotionally and/or physically close to others — especially as they become increasingly important to you.

~ David Schnarch

Schnarch was a pioneer in taking Murray Bowen's Family Systems Theory and applying it to couples relationships. He saw clearly that couples thrive best when they seek to enhance their own differentiation of self and avoid enmeshment. The more the couples he worked with achieved differentiation, the better their sexual relationship and overall relationship became. He broke from Bowen in believing that one can materially increase one's level of differentiation of self, and I agree. I recommend Albert Ellis' REBT approach as a key to this process, and I incorporate the thinking of both men into my *Mindful Reason* and *Differentiation of Self* Pillars of *Affirmative Intimacy*™.

Maintaining a sense of self becomes *more*, rather than less, important as the closeness and importance of your relationship grows. This runs contrary to popular thinking about how people in relationship should behave, but breaking free

James R. Fleckenstein

of this popular thinking is critical to attaining happy and sustainable relationships.

The Hack Boiled down to its essence, Schnarch's advice is straightforward: resist the "urge to merge." As we let our guard down in intimate relationships, we can drift into an unhealthy level of surrendering our essential selves. The core of *Differentiation of Self* is the ability to resist this drift, to avoid seeing it as a positive, and to encourage your partner (encourage, not *demand* or *expect*) to do likewise.

Take time to assess your degree of standing as a discrete person in your relationship, and decide if you need to work harder on being whole as an individual, rather than always acting as part of a unit. If you decide you need to work on this, discuss it with your partner and begin a joint plan for improvement.

James R. Fleckenstein

[R]elationship work, paradoxically, is a solitary project...It is not necessary, important, or even possible to work on the other person. One cannot change another person, though the temptation to try is always there. Change must come from within the self, for one's own reasons.

~ **Roberta M. Gilbert**

Gilbert worked directly with Bowen and is a leading practitioner of his Family Systems Theory. We see here that she shares his emphasis (which I also unreservedly support) on working only on yourself. Trying to change your partner directly is a complete and utter waste of time and energy better spent on your own development. Of course, many of us do give in to the temptation to try, usually with disastrous results!

The amazing and important thing is that, by changing *yourself*, you *do* change your partner; whether because they choose to change themselves in response to your development, or because your development causes you to see them in a new light. But right reasons have a critical role, as Gilbert notes. You must undertake *Differentiation of Self* simply because doing so benefits your own growth and well-being. The many other benefits you will experience in relationship and in life come as a *result*, not as a cause.

The Hack

As noted in the preceding action step and elsewhere in this book, Gilbert gently restates the essential truth that you can only attain these goals by and for yourself. When it comes to changing your partner – *fuhgeddaboudit!* Next time you find yourself trying to reshape your partner, stop, step back, and reconsider. Try reframing the issue as, "What can I change about *myself* that might either enable my partner to change or enable me to live at peace with them exactly as they are?" It's the answer to *that* question that sets forth your course of action. More importantly, it's a course of action that you can actually accomplish, measure your progress toward, and benefit from completing, whether your partner ever changes a bit!

Care about what other people think and you will always be their prisoner.

~ Lao Tzu

This ancient quote is a most fitting way to end this book. At the end of the day, the only person to whom you are 100% accountable is yourself. You cannot hide from yourself; you cannot (for long) lie to yourself. I'd insert "too much" into this quote, but that represents a compromise that may not be a good idea. Still, barring a serious personality disorder, if you strive to be able to face yourself in the mirror each day with equanimity, chances are you won't be held in scorn by others—at least not by those who truly matter.

Integrity comes from within, not from without. You surrender your essence as a human being every time you choose inauthentic beliefs, thoughts, or actions solely because you perceive those to be preferred by others. Do not mistake this thinking for mere callousness, or blind indifference to the feelings or beliefs of others with whom you interact. Rather, it is a conscious choice to weigh all factors, do a "gut check" for your personal integrity, and act in ways that free you from the shackles of conformity for its own sake, or because it is the path of least resistance.

James R. Fleckenstein

The competing values of social conformity and individual autonomy are locked in a never-ending struggle within most of us. We want to fit in, be liked and loved, avoid social disapproval, and avoid strife. Yet we equally want to be free to think and act as we choose, within the bounds of sensible laws. I tend to come down on the side of authenticity and autonomy, or at the very least I advocate a more favorable ratio tilted toward autonomy. Lao Tzu's choice of words is not accidental; if pleasing others is our uppermost concern, we are truly little more than prisoners of others' good will.

The Hack

The final action step involves resolving to stop being a prisoner of external expectations and the fickle, ever-changing attitudes of others. This is not to suggest an anarchistic, me-first approach to life. Nothing contained herein involves a callous disregard for the common sense rules of social interaction and civil order! What I do encourage, however, is cultivating the ability—a *learned* ability—to assess matters based on a well-considered internal compass, and acting accordingly. Absent pathology, this practice will typically result in both you and those with whom you interact having a happier, richer, and more genuine life!

If you've found this book at all helpful, I strongly recommend that you join my low-traffic mailing list by going to https://www.subscribepage.com/d3a3i9. Once you've done that, you'll be kept informed of my upcoming trainings and events, and receive my periodic newsletter.

James R. Fleckenstein

Your next steps

———— ♥ ————

I hope you have found this book useful. The concepts and practices I discuss here are applicable to all types of relationships. As noted previously, while it's *not* essential for you to have completed my training to use these ideas effectively, your chances of success increase dramatically if you have! The skills I teach give you the specific tools to accomplish your dream of an improved relationship and a more contented, happier life.

I recommend that you take a quick look at my website, www.affirmativeintimacy.com. You'll find more information there, along with an opportunity to join my mailing list. Once you've done that, you'll be kept informed of my trainings and receive my periodic newsletter.

Thank you for reading my book! I hope you enjoyed it as much as I enjoyed writing it. Won't you please consider leaving a review on Amazon? Even just a few words would help others decide if the book is right for them, and it's really important to me as well.

I've made it super simple: just type the URL below into your browser and you'll travel straight to the Amazon review page for this book where you can leave your review.

Best regards and thank you in advance:

http://www.Amazon.com/gp/customer-reviews/write-a-review.html?asin= 9781733039406

The Worksheets

I hope these worksheets will help you implement the Hacks I offer here. If you'd like full color, fillable PDF's for your own use, just go to the private web page exclusively for buyers of this book, the *Love That Works* Resources page at https://wp.me/P5us9K-9H

James R. Fleckenstein

From page 29

"SHOOTING THE MESSENGER"

DATE I COMPLETED:

THIS WORKSHEET WILL HELP YOU CAPTURE A TIME WHEN YOU PUNISHED YOUR PARTNER FOR BEING HONEST, AND THE FEELINGS INVOLVED. IT WILL ALSO HELP YOU CONSIDER OTHER APPROACHES FOR THE FUTURE.

WHEN DID IT HAPPEN?

WHAT WAS THE SUBJECT?

HOW I FELT AT THE TIME

HOW MY PARTNER MAY HAVE FELT AT THE TIME

DID I ENCOURAGE FUTURE HONESTY?

HOW I CAN DO IT DIFFERENTLY

From page 33

"ON DIFFERENT WORLDS"

DATE I COMPLETED:

THIS WORKSHEET WILL HELP YOU CAPTURE A TIME WHEN YOU JUMPED TO
CONCLUSIONS WITHOUT DUE CONSIDERATION, AND THE FEELINGS INVOLVED.
IT WILL ALSO HELP YOU CONSIDER OTHER APPROACHES FOR THE FUTURE.

WHEN DID IT HAPPEN?

WHAT WAS THE SUBJECT?

WHAT WAS THE RESULT OF YOUR ACTIONS?

DID YOU LIKE THAT OUTCOME?

IS THIS A RECURRING CHALLENGE FOR YOU?

HOW I CAN DO IT DIFFERENTLY.

James R. Fleckenstein

From page 45

WITHDRAWING

Date I completed: _____

DESCRIBE A MAJOR DISAGREEMENT YOU HAD WITH YOUR PARTNER:

WHAT FEELINGS RESULTED FROM THAT DISAGREEMENT?

CONNECTION ---|---|---|---|---|---|---|---|---|---|--- DISTANCE

IF IT PRODUCED DISTANCING, WHAT WERE YOUR REASONS?

UPON REFLECTION, WHAT DO YOU THINK OF THOSE REASONS NOW?

GOING FORWARD, HOW WILL YOU REACT DIFFERENTLY?

From page 49

TACT VS. DECEPTION

DATE I COMPLETED:

THIS WORKSHEET HELPS YOU EXPLORE THE DIFFERENCE BETWEEN TACT AND DECEPTION, AND WAYS TO IMPROVE IN THIS AREA

MERRIAM-WEBSTER DEFINITIONS

TACT:
'A KEEN SENSE OF WHAT TO DO OR SAY IN ORDER TO MAINTAIN GOOD RELATIONS WITH OTHERS OR AVOID OFFENSE'

DECEPTION:
'THE ACT OF CAUSING SOMEONE TO ACCEPT AS TRUE OR VALID WHAT IS FALSE OR INVALID'

THE DIFFERENCE IN YOUR OWN WORDS

LIST SOME SITUATIONS WHERE YOU COULD PRACTICE TACT

WHEN WAS A TIME YOU COULD HAVE BEEN TACTFUL RATHER THAN DECEPTIVE?

HOW DID YOU FEEL WHEN YOU SUBSTITUED DECEPTION FOR TACTFULNESS?

HOW DO YOU PLAN TO GAIN MORE TACT GOING FORWARD?

James R. Fleckenstein

From page 53

"I don't want to hear it!"

Date I completed:

A time when you shut down someone else...

What happened?

A time when someone shut you down...

What happened?

What will you do differently?

From page 61

WITHHOLDING

Date I completed: _____

THINK OF A TIME SOMEBODY WITHHELD INFORMATION FROM YOU:

WHAT FEELINGS RESULTED FROM THAT CHOICE? (MARK ON THE SCALE)

CLOSENESS ---|---|---|---|---|---|---|---|---|---|--- DISTANCE

DISCORD ---|---|---|---|---|---|---|---|---|---|--- HARMONY

HOW DID YOU FEEL ABOUT THEIR MOTIVATIONS?

THINK OF A TIME WHEN YOU WERE THE WITHHOLDER:

WHAT WAS YOUR RATIONALE AT THE TIME?

WHAT DO YOU THINK OF THAT RATIONALE NOW?

HOW WILL YOU CHANGE & ENLIST YOUR PARTNER'S INVOLVEMENT?

James R. Fleckenstein

From page 65

SPEAKING YOUR TRUTH

DATE I COMPLETED:

LET'S EXPLORE HOW FEAR AFFECTS YOUR WILLINGNESS TO BE TRUTHFUL
AND WHAT YOU MIGHT DO DIFFERENTLY

DESCRIBE A TIME WHEN YOU FELT AFRAID TO BE TRUTHFUL

HOW DID YOU FEEL ABOUT HAVING TO WITHHOLD YOUR TRUTH?

DO YOU WANT TO HAVE THOSE FEELINGS AGAIN?

WHAT EXACTLY WERE YOU AFRAID OF AT THE TIME?

LOOKING BACK ON THIS EVENT, WAS THAT FEAR JUSTIFIED?

WHAT WILL YOU WILL DO DIFFERENTLY GOING FORWARD?

From page 85

DID I HEAR YOU?

A WORKSHEET FOR IDENTIFYING
COMMUNICATIONS CHALLENGES

DATE I COMPLETED:

CONVERSATION TOPIC:

DATE OF CONVERSATION:

TIME OF DAY:

PARTNER'S POINT #1

WRITE KEY WORDS HERE

PARTNER'S POINT #2

WRITE KEY WORDS HERE

PARTNER'S POINT #3

WRITE KEY WORDS HERE

PARTNER'S POINT #4

WRITE KEY WORDS HERE

James R. Fleckenstein

From page 89

DID YOU HEAR ME?
A WORKSHEET FOR IDENTIFYING
COMMUNICATIONS CHALLENGES

DATE I COMPLETED:

CONVERSATION TOPIC:

DATE OF CONVERSATION:

TIME OF DAY:

POINT #1
WRITE KEY WORDS HERE

POINT #2
WRITE KEY WORDS HERE

POINT #3
WRITE KEY WORDS HERE

POINT #4
WRITE KEY WORDS HERE

From page 105

IRRECONCILABLE DIFFERENCES

IDENTIFYING WHAT CAN AND CAN'T BE CHANGED IN YOUR RELATIONSHIP

DATE I COMPLETED: _____

Researcher John Gottman discovered, over a lifetime of research, that there are about 10 issues in every relationship that are simply irreconcilable. Arguing about these is an utter waste of time. Yet people persist in doing just that - for decades in some cases! Use this worksheet (one for each of you) to list (privately) what bothers you the most in your relationship (behaviors, habits, expressions, approaches, etc.). It could be something you wish would *start* happening or *stop* happening. List as many as you like - then narrow them down to the "top 10" once you're done. Just fill in the blanks with what comes to you to complete this sentence, *"I really wish my partner would..."* If you need more space, write on the back!

James R. Fleckenstein

From page 109

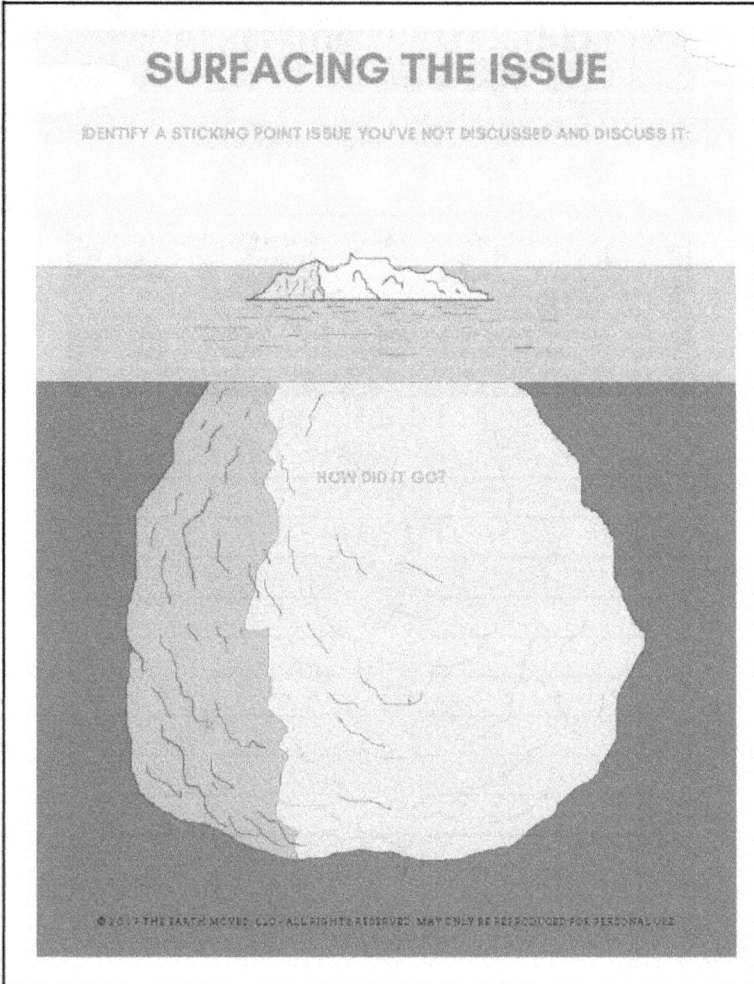

From page 131

TAKING ACTION NOW

Date I completed:

First Relationship Concern:

What you're going to do about it THIS WEEK:

Second Relationship Concern:

What you're going to do about it THIS WEEK:

Third Relationship Concern:

What you're going to do about it THIS WEEK:

James R. Fleckenstein

From page 163

Changing Your Partner

Fill out one worksheet for each of five characteristics of your partner that you wish you could change

What I wish I could change about my partner:

_____

_____

_____

Was this characteristic evident early in our relationship?

_____

_____

Have I ever discussed this characteristic with my partner? What happened?

_____

_____

_____

How would our relationship be different if this characteristic changed in the way I'd prefer?

_____

_____

_____

Why I think our relationship would be better if this changed:

_____

_____

Would this change result in my partner being more like me?

_____

_____

If yes, why, specifically, would that be a good thing?

_____

_____

From page 175

(UN)ESSENTIAL SACRIFICES

GIVING UP ESSENTIAL PARTS OF YOURSELF

Date:

Directions: In the left column, list up to three practices, beliefs, or attitudes that you felt compelled to sacrifice "for the sake of your relationship," whether or not anyone made explicit demands or requests that you do so. In the corresponding right column, capture how it felt or feels to you to no longer have access to those practices, beliefs, or attitudes.

1.) What I sacrificed:

How I felt/feel about it:

2.) What I sacrificed:

How I felt/feel about it:

3.) What I sacrificed:

How I felt/feel about it:

Three things I expected my partner to sacrifice "for the sake of the relationship":

James R. Fleckenstein

Chapter Notes

Chapter One

1. Abdel-Tawab, R., James, D. H., Fichtinger, A., Clatworthy, J., Horne, R., & Davies, G. (2011). Development and validation of the medication-related consultation framework (MRCF). *Patient education and counseling, 83*(3), 451-457.

2. Baile, W. F., Buckman, R., Lenzi, R., Glober, G., Beale, E. A., & Kudelka, A. P. (2000). SPIKES—a six-step protocol for delivering bad news: application to the patient with cancer. *The oncologist, 5*(4), 302-311.

3. Lepp, M., & Zorn, C. R. (2002). Life circle: Creating safe space for educational empowerment. *Journal of Nursing Education, 41*(9), 383-385.

Chapter Two

1. Hendrix, H. (2007). *Getting the love you want: A guide for couples.* St. Martin's Griffin. (p. 142-154)

2. Leaper, C., & Ayres, M. M. (2007). A meta-analytic review of gender variations in adults' language use: Talkativeness, affiliative speech, and assertive speech. *Personality and Social Psychology Review*, 11(4), 328-363.

3. Dudley, R., Taylor, P., Wickham, S., & Hutton, P. (2015). Psychosis, delusions and the "jumping to conclusions" reasoning bias: a systematic

review and meta-analysis. *Schizophrenia bulletin, 42*(3), 652-665.

4.https://lindaklaffey.com/irreconcilable-differences/

Chapter Three

1. Ellis, A. (1962). *Reason and emotion in psychotherapy.* New York: Lyle Stewart.

2. Greene, R. R., & Graham, S. A. (2009). Role of resilience among Nazi Holocaust survivors: A strength-based paradigm for understanding survivorship. *Family & community health, 32*(1), S75-S82.

Chapter Four

1. Fischer, T. F. (2004, October). Self-Differentiation: An Essential Attitude For Healthy Leadership. *Ministry Health Newsletter.* Retrieved from http://www.ministryhealth.net/mh_articles/34 5_self_differ_essential_healthy_church.html

2. Peleg, O. (2008). The relation between differentiation of self and marital satisfaction: What can be learned from married people over the course of life?. *The American Journal of Family Therapy, 36*(5), 388-401.

3. Holman, T. B., & Busby, D. M. (2011). Family-of-origin, differentiation of self and partner, and adult romantic relationship quality. *Journal of Couple & Relationship Therapy, 10*(1), 3-19.

4. Gabelman, E. (2012). *The effects of locus of control and differentiation of self on relationship satisfaction.* (Doctoral dissertation, The Ohio State University).

5. Ferreira, L. C., Narciso, I., Novo, R. F., & Pereira, C. R. (2014). Predicting couple satisfaction: The role of differentiation of self, sexual desire and intimacy in heterosexual individuals. *Sexual and Relationship Therapy, 29*(4), 390-404.

6. Kalmijn, M. (2003). Friendship Networks over the Life Course: A test of the Dyadic Withdrawal Hypothesis Using Survey Data on Couples. *Social Networks, 25*(3), 231-249.

7. Johnson, M. P., & Leslie, L. (1982). Couple involvement and network structure: A test of the dyadic withdrawal hypothesis. *Psychology Quarterly, 45*(1), 34-43.

8. Burton-Chellew, M. N., & Dunbar, R. I. M. (2015). Romance and reproduction are socially costly. *Evolutionary Behavioral Sciences, 9*(4), 229-241.

9. Shackelford, T. K., Goetz, A. T., McKibbin, W. F., & Starratt, V. G. (2007). Absence makes the adaptations grow fonder: Proportion of time apart from partner, male sexual psychology, and sperm competition in humans (Homo sapiens). *Journal of Comparative Psychology, 121*(2), 214.

10. Starratt, V. G., McKibbin, W. F., & Shackelford, T. K. (2013). Experimental

activation of anti-cuckoldry mechanisms responsive to female sexual infidelity. *Personality and Individual Differences, 55*(1), 59-62.

11. Shackelford, T., & Goetz, A. (2009). Sexual conflict in humans: Evolutionary consequences of asymmetric parental investment and paternity uncertainty. *Animal Biology, 59*(4), 449-456.

About the Author

Like many others, Jim Fleckenstein became a relationship coach and educator because of his own life experiences. After the end of his 25-year marriage in 2000, he put the skills he'd gained from his successful non-profit career and his insatiable curiosity to work on relationships. He created an educational non-profit to foster new research into relationships. He also began a rigorous self-education process that included reaching out personally to leading researchers.

His efforts quickly bore fruit. His organization ultimately conducted five national conferences on relationships. He was invited to co-present for the first time before the American Association of Sexuality Educators, Counselors and Therapists (AASECT) in 2002. He has since been invited to present at seven more AASECT conferences, to the Eastern Region Conference of the Society for the Scientific Study of Sexuality, to the Society for Sex Therapy and Research, and to the American Association for Marriage and Family Therapy. He was invited to contribute to the *Continuum Complete International Encyclopedia of Sexuality* in 2004. In 2015, he was lead author on his first published research paper in the peer-reviewed journal, *Sexual and Relationship Therapy*. This paper was selected to become a chapter in the 2015 book, *Sexuality and Aging*.

He merged his organization into another, larger group in 2006 so as to continue his focus on self-education, scientific research, and helping people have successful relationships. In addition to his professional presentations, Jim became a regular volunteer presenter at lay conferences, with nearly 20 appearances.

Along the way, Jim developed a unique philosophical approach to relationships based on methods he encountered over the years. Ultimately this crystallized into his ***Affirmative Intimacy*™** method. He created The Earth Moved, LLC in 2012 as a professional home for his coaching and educational efforts.

About the Sources

Alan Alda (1936-) American actor, director, author and activist.

Pietro Aretino (1492-1556) Italian poet, prose writer, and dramatist.

Kelli Jae Baeli (1962-) American bestselling novelist (33 titles), independent publisher, editor, webmaster, blogger, artist, and singer-songwriter, with over 200 songwriting credits.

Ambrose Bierce (1842-1914) American editorialist, journalist, short-story writer, fabulist, and satirist.

Murray Bowen, M.D. (1913-1990) American psychiatrist and professor, creator of the Family Systems psychiatric theory.

Robert Brault (1938-) American freelance writer and author who has contributed to magazines and newspapers in the USA for over 40 years.

Jeff Daly American architect, exhibit designer, museum consultant, and designer of new museum galleries.

Miles Davis (1926-1991) American jazz musician, trumpeter, bandleader, and composer.

Wayne Dyer, Ph.D. (1940-2015) American self-help author and motivational speaker.

Epictetus (55-135) A Greek-speaking Stoic philosopher, born in what is now Turkey.

Robert E. Fisher (1940-) Author and historian.

Khalil Gibran (1883-1931) Lebanese-American artist, poet, and writer.

Roberta M. Gilbert, M.D. American psychiatrist whose special interest is Bowen Family Systems theory and its extensions and applications to individuals, families, and organizations.

Henepola Gunaratana (1927-) A Sri Lankan Theravada Buddhist monk.

Criss Jami (1987-) An American poet, essayist, existentialist philosopher, songwriter, and the creator/designer of Killosopher Apparel.

Samuel Johnson (1709-1784) English poet, essayist, moralist, literary critic, biographer, editor and lexicographer.

Byron Katie (1942-) American speaker and author.

Stephan Labossiere (1978-) American certified relationship coach, speaker and author.

Lao Tzu (?-531 BCE) A philosopher and poet of ancient China. He is known as the reputed author of the *Tao Te Ching* and the founder of philosophical Taoism.

Anne Morrow Lindbergh (1906-2001) American author, aviator, and the wife of fellow aviator Charles Lindbergh.

Audre Lorde (1934-1992) Caribbean-American writer, radical feminist, womanist, lesbian, and civil rights activist.

Thomas Merton (1915-1968) American Catholic writer, Trappist monk and mystic.

Joel Osteen (1963-) American minister, televangelist, author, and the Senior Pastor of Lakewood Church, the largest Protestant church in the United States, in Houston, Texas.

Robert Quillen (1887-1948) American journalist and humorist.

Rainer Maria Rilke (1875-1926) Bohemian-Austrian poet and novelist.

Tony Robbins (1960-) American motivational speaker, personal finance instructor, and self-help author.

Leo Rosten (1908-1997) Polish-born American humorist, scriptwriter and journalist.

Don Miguel Ruiz (1952-) A Mexican author of Toltec spiritualist and neoshamanistic texts.

May Sarton (1912-1995) American poet, novelist and memoirist.

David Schnarch, Ph.D. (1946-) American licensed clinical psychologist and author of numerous books and articles on intimacy, sexuality, and relationships.

George Bernard Shaw (1856-1950) Nobel Prize-winning Irish playwright, critic and passionate socialist.

Simon Sinek (1973-) English author, ethnographer and leadership expert.

Douglas Stone American author, founder of Triad Consulting and a Lecturer on Law at Harvard Law School.

W. Clement Stone (1902-2002) American businessman, philanthropist and New Thought self-help book author.

Tacitus (56-117) Roman senator and historian.

Susan Wheelan, Ph.D. American psychologist, professor and author.

Oscar Wilde (1854-1900) Irish playwright, novelist, essayist and poet.

Recommended Reading

You should know that as an Amazon Associate, I earn from qualifying purchases. If you type in the provided URL to a product and buy it, I will receive a small commission, which helps further my work. I only recommend resources that I genuinely believe will help you, and buying through my link does not increase what you pay for the item(s).

Structured Dialog

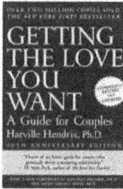

Getting the Love You Want: A Guide for Couples, 20th Anniversary Edition

(https://amzn.to/2LWn7to)

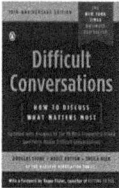

Difficult Conversations: How to Discuss What Matters Most

(https://www.amazon.to/2LAz1Kx)

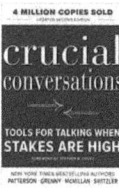

Crucial Conversations: Tools for Talking When Stakes Are High, Second Edition

(https://www.amazon.to/32ORKb4)

James R. Fleckenstein

Mindful Reason

A Guide to Rational Living
(https://amzn.to/32MzTRR/)

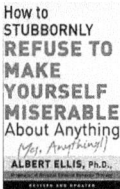

How To Stubbornly Refuse To Make Yourself Miserable About Anything-yes, Anything!
(https://amzn.to/2O7yr8Q)

How to Keep People from Pushing Your Buttons
(https://amzn.to/307SxXx)

Sex Without Guilt in the Twenty-First Century
(https://amzn.to/31vgxRb/)

A Guide to Successful Marriage
(https://amzn.to/2QhzeGN)

Overcoming Jealousy and Possessiveness

(https://amzn.to/32KEQe3/)

Differentiation of Self

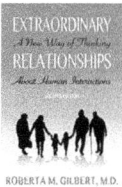

Extraordinary Relationships: A New Way of Thinking about Human Interactions, Second Edition

(https://amzn.to/3064soZ/)

The Eight Concepts of Bowen Theory

(https://amzn.to/309xlzu)

Passionate Marriage: Keeping Love and Intimacy Alive in Committed Relationships

(https://amzn.to/2LCBV1j/)

Order Form

Can't find it in the bookstore? You can order print copies of *Love That Works: 38 Awesome Hacks for Amazing Relationships* directly from the publisher using this form. They make great gifts for anyone you may know who wants a happier and more authentic relationship—newlyweds, about-to-be-weds, people in long-term relationships that could use a boost—pretty much anyone!

Number of books _____

Total Cost of books @ $11.99 $_____
(Inquire about bulk discounts for 10 or more copies)

Shipping & Handling: 10% of total order (min $5.00)
$_____

Subtotal with shipping $_____

Virginia residents please add 6% sales tax $_____

TOTAL $_____

METHOD OF PAYMENT:

___ Check enclosed, payable to **The Earth Moved, LLC**

___ VISA ___ MC

Card # _____
Expiration____/____/____

Signature: _____
CVV_____

James R. Fleckenstein

BILLING ADDRESS (MUST MATCH CREDIT CARD):

Name: _____

Address: _____

City: _____

State: _____ ZIP Code: _____

Phone: _____

Email: _____

SHIP TO ADDRESS (if different from Billing Address):

Name: _____

Address: _____

City: _____

State: _____ ZIP Code: _____

Phone: _____

Email: _____

MAIL OR EMAIL THIS FORM TO:

THE EARTH MOVED, LLC

8665 Sudley Road, #132
Manassas, VA 20110
books@affirmativeintimacy.com

No orders can be shipped without full payment received in advance. Orders will be shipped promptly upon payment, via US. Mail or UPS/FedEx ground, depending on weight.

www.ingramcontent.com/pod-product-compliance
Lightning Source LLC
Chambersburg PA
CBHW070923030426
42336CB00014BA/2507